...d Technology
...ertainment

Media Design and Technology for Live Entertainment is a guide to understanding the concepts and equipment used in projection and video design for live performances. After an introduction in the principles of design elements as well as information on content, this book focuses on how content is used and transmitted by describing the essential components of systems, providing definitions used in communicating video concepts, and including basic system troubleshooting tips and tricks. A brief history of projected imagery is included, as well as information on analog systems, as outdated technology continues to be used either by choice of the designer or by necessity due to budget. By providing the information to understand the tools and how to use them, the reader should be able to create their own systems to meet his or her design ideas.

Davin E. Gaddy has been working professionally in live entertainment, convention and trade show, themed exhibit, and cinema markets for over 25 years, not including his prior student work. During this time, he has spanned the gamut of the industry, learning a variety of production styles. Due to his experience, Gaddy was the perfect fit to be the lead projectionist for Cirque du Soleil's production of *KÀ*, which has stunned millions of audience members over the course of its run.

In addition, Gaddy advocates for the education of other members of the industry. He has taught workshops on video for performance at theatrical conventions, as well as directly to students at high schools, colleges, and universities. Gaddy serves as a moderator on ControlBooth.com, an online forum for the theatrical industry. Gaddy is the chairman of the committee preparing the video and projection exam for USITT's Essential Skills for the Entertainment Technician program.

Media Design and Technology for Live Entertainment

Essential Tools for Video Presentation

Davin E. Gaddy

Routledge
Taylor & Francis Group

NEW YORK AND LONDON

First published 2018
by Routledge
711 Third Avenue, New York, NY 10017

and by Routledge
2 Park Square, Milton Park, Abingdon, Oxon, OX14 4RN

Routledge is an imprint of the Taylor & Francis Group, an informa business

Library of Congress Cataloging-in-Publication Data
A catalog record for this book has been requested

ISBN: 978-1-138-21513-9 (hbk)
ISBN: 978-1-138-21621-1 (pbk)
ISBN: 978-1-315-44272-3 (ebk)

Typeset in ITC Giovanni Std
by Keystroke, Neville Lodge, Tettenhall, Wolverhampton

To my wife and family, who have patiently
supported me through this journey.

Contents

Contents

Contents

x

Contents

Acknowledgments

Learning about video for live performance is often a challenge, and the ability to teach others required the assistance of some great associates. I would like to thank (in no particular order) Ahmednur "OZ" Osman, Brad Weber, Jacob Pinholster, Wendall Harrington, Alex Oliszewski, and the countless engineers whom I have met at various trade shows. I would also like to thank the media designers who have silently inspired me to learn more about this field.

CHAPTER 1

Introduction

In the simultaneous use of the living actor and the talking picture in the theater there lies a wholly new theatrical art, whose possibilities are as infinite as those of speech itself.

~Robert Edmond Jones

PURPOSE

Many directors and producers have found that they want to have the latest techniques to have their production be cutting edge. They often make the decision that adding projection will take their production to the next level. This text is not designed to help make the decision on whether or not this will add value to the production. Instead, it will offer insight into the planning and preparation of the media experience in order to integrate it in the best possible way. As those who are making the decisions are often aware of their own consumer experience (home theater), as well as being influenced by what they have seen as possible, there can be a misunderstanding of what is necessary to make a great performance. No one piece of the model will make the system great, but missing an element could make it nonfunctional.

This text will teach about the parts of the system to give the design team the understanding of how to get started. Just as any artist or craftsman needs to understand the tools and materials that he or she will use to create their art, the projection designer needs to understand the tools and materials at his or her disposal. There is no right way to create art, but there can be methods and techniques which can be improved upon. Just as the great masters of previous arts did not produce masterpieces on their first try, the new media designer must also understand that this will take time to perfect, to learn the nuances of the media. The limitation of tools does not mean that great work cannot be created, either; rather, it offers a challenge to be worked through.

As a mechanic learns the components of an internal combustion engine, so will a media designer need to understand the individual components of a media system. There are many different types and sizes of engines, from the humble lawn mower to the highly tuned sports car, but they all fall within the same principles of physics. A highly skilled mechanic may be able to work on many different engines, but there will be parts that may require special knowledge or tools as well as the knowledge on how to tune any specific component. As such, this will not be a manual for a specific engine, but a knowledge base to aid in figuring out the specifics of the system you need and the general knowledge of how they work in order to build an engine that best works for you and your production.

Projection and Media Design
In his work *The Dramatic Imagination*, Robert Edmond Jones, a renowned scenic designer, mused on the desire of playwrights to have a dreamlike quality in productions and the dissonance of the moving picture. While it was a challenge in the early twentieth century, today it is a movement in its own right. Projection design has become a catchphrase for the technique of using images created with light for performance; most often they are being projected. This is the designation by IATSE local

829, the United Scenic Artists branch of the International Association of Theatrical Stage Employees, Moving Picture Technicians, Artists and Allied Crafts (IATSE). However, in this text, the term *projection design* will be used only when projectors will be the display technology. There are a variety of technologies which are covered under *media design* in addition to the projector; these include LED panels and video monitors and others still under development, as well as classic single image projection devices. This book will provide the designer with the knowledge necessary to understand the various principles and components of a video system, in order to present a visually stunning performance.

Characteristics

In media design, there are common characteristics, as well as distinct differences, in the image and how it is displayed. It is ephemeral, meaning that it is not wholly tangible. It can replicate scenic painting in some aspects, which helped it to gain prominence and is likely to be the motivation for its first use for a production company. It is mutable; thus it only needs to be seen when necessary, at a moment's notice. As with painting techniques, there are different textures created. There are differences between film media with its inherent grain and the pixel data of a digitally projected image. Also, what the image is projected on can have extreme effects on the resultant image as well as the technology to create the pixel.

Aesthetic, cultural, dramaturgical, and ethical considerations of transposing images and live actors must be determined on a case by case basis for the overall design. Some considerations include legality, in terms of Actors Equity and Screen Actors Guild actors, for the process of recording and playback. The media design needs to address intellectual property ownership of images through copyright and trademarks. If performances are distributed, it needs to address any possible change of

3

FIGURE 1.1

Some example designs.

Source: Wendall Harrington

FIGURE 1.2
Another example, some miss the mark.

5

restrictions. Additionally, the design authorship between the selections of images used for playback versus purposeful creation of imagery during the performance needs to be defined. Also, the relative size and visual impact of the elements, along with the nature of the performance, will have an impact on the design. Therefore, the designer needs to understand the relationship between the actor and the image.

Classification

It has often been written that the theatrical use of this technology is a "convergence" of media. In other industries where this technology is used, there is a distinction in defining its place as its own entity; this is not necessarily so in the performance world. While this may only be necessary when the design is up for an award, new production companies might want to know where media design fits within the general realm of established companies.

Since it is used as a scenic element most often, some choose to have projection as a part of carpentry and its associated departments, with some elements needing to be rigged as well. As it is a light source, some companies choose to have it be a part of a lighting department. This often makes sense in many music venues where the media servers are controlled by a lighting console. On the other hand, some will place it with the audio department. This may seem very unlikely, but audio has traditionally been in charge of in-house video for years through the responsibility for closed circuit television (CCTV). Also, many of the audio playback systems are easily adapted for video playback as well. Finally, there are some who feel that it needs to be on its own, which could be unnecessary depending on the production needs. In all, it truly depends on the needs of each individual production or company as to how media design fills their needs.

A BRIEF HISTORY

While media design is not new, it has come to the forefront of the public's recognition at the dawn of the twenty-first century. Social media has allowed the sharing of experiences at concerts and special events where structures come to life with light. In addition, with great advancements in technology, it is much easier to take the show on the road, so to speak, allowing audiences all over the world the opportunity to see visual performances which would have been either too expensive or time-consuming to accomplish in the past. It all began as a means of telling stories and it will continue to do so by more eloquent means; as the projected image has been used to provide visual magic, it has once again become a mainstay due in part to its renewed popularity.

Light and Shadow

Storytelling has been a part of human culture since long before the written word. We do not know when the storyteller chose to go beyond just an auditory presentation by adding visual elements, but we do know that it happened. At some point, people found that we can form shadows into shapes that resemble something wholly different than that which created them, such as rabbits and wolves, with nothing other than a light and their hands. Even then there was a desire to enhance the performance and they advanced technology to using a surface, which allowed light to pass through it while using two-dimensional puppets to manipulate the light. This art is still practiced to this day in some cultures. These methods both allow for movement and change in the projected image, but are limited in showing a connection to the medium creating them. Thus various projectors were invented, resembling what we know in lighting.

FIGURE 1.3
Examples of shadow projection.

Source: Shutterstock

SINGLE IMAGE PROJECTORS

Shadows were the primary method of early visual design, even beyond shadow puppetry. Single image projectors are items that have been adopted by theatrical lighting designs and are commonly associated with them in modern design. This is the method of projection which places a medium between the light source and some surface, with the possibility of lenses for focusing the image. In the theater, these are commonly known as gobos, or templates, used in an ellipsoidal reflector spotlight (commonly known as a Leko or Source Four) as part of lighting design. These are most often made of a cut metal, but they can be made of a transparent substrate with a colored pattern printed on them or even textured glass.

FIGURE 1.4
A metal gobo, its projected image, and its digital representation.

There have been several different devices made specifically for the purpose of projecting an image throughout the history of performance. Some of these have had a long-lasting history of developments while others faded into obscurity fairly quickly. Only those which have had developments leading to modernity will be mentioned.

Magic Lantern

The magic lantern is a device created in the seventeenth century (with roots from the fifteenth century) and was used to project an image that was painted on glass, with the purpose of representing the supernatural, particularly the devil or other demons. This likely represents a critical association with the desire to purposefully use light to trick an audience into truly believing and not simply suspending disbelief during a performance. As the light source was not initially very powerful, strict control of ambient light was crucial to the success of the effect.

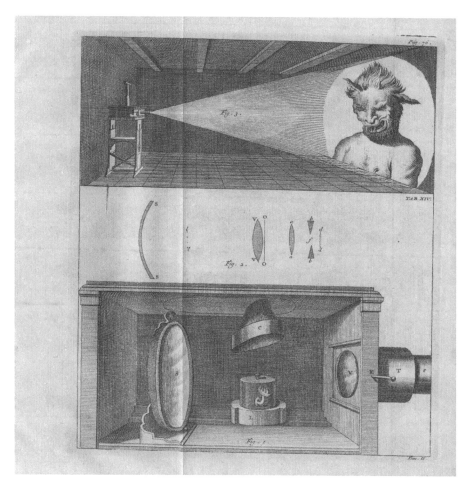

FIGURE 1.5
Use of the magic lantern.

Source: Max Planck Institute for the History of Science, Berlin

This was a simple device consisting of a light source within a box, containing a reflector which directed the light through a framed medium out the lens. As better light sources were invented, including those which had the capability of dimming, there was a surge of more creative uses of this type of device, including experimenting with transitions between devices, using them to create movement and finding new surfaces to project upon to create different effects. This became a popular European pastime in performances known as phantasmagoria.

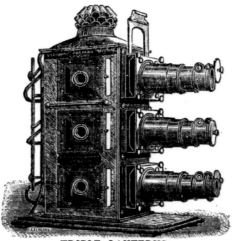

FIGURE 1.6

Advertisement for advanced magic lantern.

Source: Colonial and Indian Exhibition 1886, Public Domain

Successors of this device are many, based on the same principle, which include the Linnebach (non-focusing) projector, slide projectors, and the previously mentioned pattern placed in a theatrical spotlight.

Slide Projector

As the modern equivalent to the magic lantern, the slide projector offered many new benefits. Slides became printed on a film medium, allowing for the greater ability of duplication (backup copies or for multiple productions). Slide projectors were made with a variety of trays, allowing for switching images easily. The switching of images was noisy and was abrupt. Later optical improvements included asymmetrical lenses, allowing for the projector to be off axis and prevent keystoning of the image. Additional advancements allowed for a dissolve of the image. This included control of multiple projectors, allowing for a smooth transition.

FIGURE 1.7
Stacked slide projectors.

Source: kxcamera.com

Transitioning between multiple stacked projectors was still a viable production element into the late twentieth century. Broadway productions such as *The Who's Tommy*, designed by Wendall Harrington, used dozens of slide projectors for the visuals. At least two projectors could be aligned to a single screen where specialized control units would fade between projectors.

Large-format versions of the slide projector, manufactured by companies such as Pani and Pigi, were adopted as early as the mid-1950s and offered the brightest available projection at the time. The original units were based on high brightness Xenon lamps used in searchlights. They can be used with single slides, while some are fitted with scrolling media allowing for either multiple still images or gently rotating images. A single projector can illuminate the entire side of a large building or even a side of a mountain, but the output is not yet viable when using individual digital projectors.

12

Film Projector

Throughout the development of the magic lantern the ability to change the image was invented, but speed and fluidity of the change was limited. With the advent of flexible film medium, the Lumiere brothers introduced a new staple to performance: the film projector. The difficulty for production companies using this technology then and throughout its use was the cost of creating the medium. It was first seen on Broadway in the 1940s, though it was used even earlier in Europe. Unfortunately, it was met with limited success as there were high costs associated with not only creating the content, but also its long-term use. It also is limited to the speed of creating the medium and the lack of adaptability as directors change their minds. In addition, there was an inherent danger that some early film stock was flammable and extremely volatile. It could be argued that there was enough desire for it as a possibility for a production that many theaters incorporated projection booths, even if they never ended up being used for anything other than storage. Long-running productions in cities like Las Vegas were still using film projectors through the first few years of the twenty-first century. At the time of publication, it is unknown if any permanent production is still using film, or if it has all been replaced by digital projection.

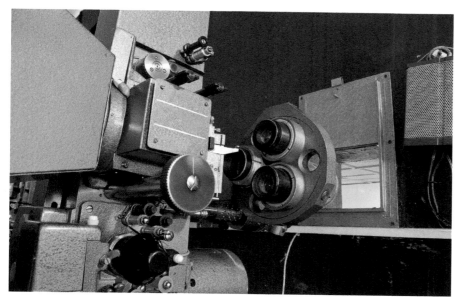

FIGURE 1.8
Film projector.

Source: Shutterstock

Video Projector

During the latter half of the twentieth century, images were being transferred to the screen without a physical image medium. Instead, analog electrical signals transferred the information to the projector. The first video projectors were Cathode Ray Tube (CRT) projectors, which had a separate lens for each of the three primary colors of light: red, green, and blue. When the projector was set up, the three lenses would have to each be aligned to the screen, converging the three colors to combine into a wide gamut of colors. Like earlier projectors, these were often not very bright and had difficulty competing with ambient light. It was a leap forward from film projectors in that a greater flexibility of content was achieved, but the lack of brightness and the difficulty in image convergence made them unpopular in almost all live performance. They required highly skilled technicians to set them up in controlled environments. Digital video projectors are in constant development and have surpassed possibly all expectations of what early designers thought possible. The ease of use and affordability has made them accessible to a greater number of productions. In order to better understand their benefits and limitations, modern video projectors will be discussed in detail in Chapter 5.

PHYSIOLOGY AND PSYCHOLOGY

Visual media is concerned only with the human sense of eyesight. Other factors must be considered when designing the system for a production, such as how loud the technology is or how much heat is produced, both of which can impact the overall production even if it does not change the quality of the image. The main concern of a media design team, beyond *what* is to be seen, is to ensure *that* the media is properly seen. If the designer is looking for a particular purple, then there will be several factors to consider in creating a color as close to that purple as possible. Thus, it is important that we understand optics—the continuing study of light.

The choice of color is often a primary concern with a visual designer. Depending on a culture, color representation can have specific meaning and may change if the color is not properly presented. Also, when working with a representation of a specific product or logo such as the color red used by

Coca-Cola, it is critical to have accurate color representation. The color choice of the corporation will actually be registered and will have a specific Pantone color designation.

The following chapters will discuss the various technologies which will aid in presenting content. For now, we will take a brief look at the physics of light, including how to manipulate it, as well as how humans perceive it.

Physics of Light

Understanding the properties of light is often the biggest challenge for the media designer in bringing designs from conception to reality. Light has been studied for centuries as to what it is and how it behaves. Fortunately, we have the benefit of all this research to understand how to use it and many engineers have provided us with the best tools to accurately create an image. To understand how to make the best image possible, we need to have a basic knowledge of these properties in order to make the most out of the tools available.

15

While the designer is primarily concerned with visible light, that part of the electromagnetic spectrum which is detectable by the human eye, he or she must also know that other spectrums may have some influence as well. The electromagnetic spectrum covers everything from the visible spectrum to radio waves, infrared, ultraviolet, X-rays, and gamma radiation. The visible spectrum covers a very narrow band, which is where all of the colors of the rainbow are present. When they combine, we see white light. Combining colors is the principle used by all digital display devices to represent the visible spectrum.

As we project light, we are primarily concerned with the physical optics, which deal with the wave properties. Light is a transverse wave which oscillates in a direction perpendicular to its travel. It travels in waves and is characterized by frequency

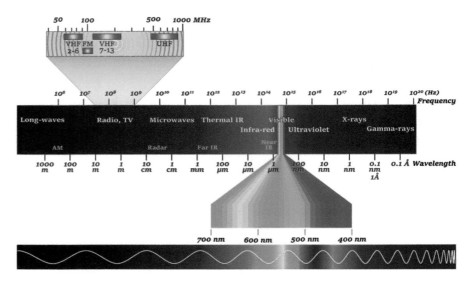

FIGURE 1.9
The electromagnetic spectrum.

Source: Shutterstock

and wavelength. The two principles we are concerned with here are interference and diffraction.

As waves interact with one another, they can change their behavior. This is known as wave propagation. Often this is seen in a resultant wave which is greater or diminished in amplitude. This intensity change appears as brighter (in-phase coherence) or darker fringes (antiphase coherence) within the image. This is especially important when we combine multiple projectors for a single image, either blended or stacked. When unstructured, light that is encountering interference can be seen in everyday phenomena such as the iridescence of a soap bubble.

Diffraction is when light encounters an obstacle and fills in some of the area behind the obstacle, which is a property also observable in mechanical waves. The interference patterns will appear as light and dark areas, known as fringes. The light that is blocked is known as a shadow. If a shadow has a sharp edge, it is known as an umbra. It is generally nearer to the surface receiving the shadow and totally blocks the light. A fuzzy edged shadow is known as penumbra, which is separated from the surface (light filling in behind it) or there are multiple sources of light or the light has been scattered. This principle will be best understood when we use shadow projection as well as Linnebach projectors.

In order to create light, scientists and engineers have learned to harness different principles. In nature, we often see light created through chemical reactions. This is how a firefly or a glowworm creates light. However, we also harness various means to create fire, which is a chemical reaction between a combustible material, oxygen, and heat. In fact, the earliest measurement of light is candle power. But we also use electricity to create light. We do this through incandescent sources, which use heat to excite a material such as a filament, which in turn can heat gasses in an envelope to radiate light. Also, the use of electricity can create luminescent sources of light, which do not provide as much heat and can be more energy efficient. As light is part of the electromagnetic spectrum, it can be shaped based on the electrical charge. This allows for optical polarization, which is useful in devices such as lasers and those which use optical encoding.

17

Light has both the properties of particles and waves, though we don't perceive both at the same time. We use geometric optics as the means of making images, which is the manipulation of the particle properties of light. For this type, we understand that light radiates from its source in a straight line. Reflection, scattering, and refraction are the primary principles in geo-metrical optics, which are precisely measured in the video projector, but are also used in presenting as well.

All physical objects we see are primarily a result of the property of reflection. Depending on the texture of a surface, the light will reflect in regular or irregular patterns. We understand that when we look into a mirror, we see a relatively complete representation of the physical object, ourselves. When we stand off to the side, we see something away from us. This deals with the angle of incidence in which the light reflects off the mirror.

When we look at the can of Coca-Cola, we see the red of its logo due to the ink which is absorbing the rest of the visible spectrum and reflecting the red. The white portion of the logo is reflecting multiple colors so that we see white. Keep in mind that an opaque object reflects all light that it does not absorb. On the other hand, a transparent object reflects little light and allows light energy to easily pass through it. However, transparent objects will refract that energy to some degree. A translucent object will allow some light to pass through it, with a great amount of scattering of the light. The thicker the translucent object is, the more opaque it becomes, while the thinner it is, the more transparent it becomes.

Specular reflection comes from a flat surface. It occurs when a surface feature height is less than the wavelength of incident light. We know this as a mirrored surface. This type of reflection can even occur on an extremely smooth surface of water. Meanwhile, a diffuse reflection comes from rough surfaces in which the surface feature height is equal to or greater than the wavelength of incident light. This reflects the light in random directions, allowing for a greater field of view, such as a page in a book.

When dealing with mirrored surfaces, we describe them in three types. The first is what most of us are used to when we look into our washroom mirror. It is a flat surface and the angle of the light incidence is equal to that of the reflection. If you were to draw a line exactly perpendicular to the surface, you would be able to see equal angles on either side of that perpendicular to predict the path of light. However, a concave surface, the second type, bends angles inwards. As it is bending inwards, it will have the effect of magnifying the image near to the surface. Some mirrors are made this way and are often referred to as makeup mirrors. However, as you get past the focal point of the mirror, the image inverts, making the image appear upside down. The final surface is convex. This bends the angles outwards, making the image smaller. Often security (domed or semi-domed) or some vehicular mirrors are made this way in order to obtain a wider angle of view in a smaller distance. Combining of mirror types can often be seen in carnival mirrors because the distortion can create fun images.

Whereas reflection occurs at a surface, another property is known as scattering, which occurs when light passes through objects without a well-defined surface, such as liquids and gasses. The light is directed in all directions, including some light which continues in the original path. There are two distinct ways that light scatters. The first is Rayleigh scattering. This is where the wavelength of light is much greater than the diameter of the particles it comes in contact with. This is most evident when we see a blue sky. The shorter wavelengths (blues) scatter

19

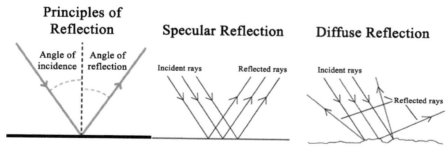

FIGURE 1.10
Principles of reflection.

more than those of longer wavelengths. However, at sunrise and sunset, we see more reds due to the fact that the light is passing through more atmosphere, scattering blues to the extent that they are seen less and also increasing the scattering of the longer wavelengths, making them more visible. The other form is known as Mie scattering. This is where the particles are similar in size to the wavelength of light or slightly larger. This has the effect of scattering incident light equally, in all directions. This is why we see milk and clouds as white. It is also why the sky appears to be a more pastel hue in more humid climates than the dry desert sky. Lighting designers take advantage of these properties by using various amounts of atmospheric effects. The media designer should remember that wavelengths with less energy and lower frequency will slow down less than the light with higher energy and higher frequency. These are the properties of dispersion and will have an effect on the resultant image.

FIGURE 1.11
Refraction in practice.

Source: Shutterstock

Refraction bends the light as it passes from one transparent medium to another. We use lenses to control light based on this principle. This gives us the ability to bring an image into focus and allows for light to spread or narrow in a zoom lens. Light changes direction as it changes from one material to another, such as air to glass. We can see this when we look at an object that is submerged in water; its shape will be distorted.

Someone driving a car may have experienced a similar reaction to refraction if they have one tire hit gravel on the side of the road (a change of one surface to another). The speed of a part of the car is slowed down by the change in medium as compared to the rest of the car, which will pull in the direction of the new material. Once the remainder of the car has fully transitioned to that new material, the car will straighten out and continue in a straight path.

Just as there are different means by which light is reflected, there are predictable ways in which it can be refracted. When dealing with lenses, we can use biconvex lenses, which have the opposite centers further out than the edges. This will bend the light inward allowing for a focal point. This is the principle used in a magnifying glass. Similar to a concave mirror, beyond the focal point, the image will invert. The other type is known as biconcave. These will have the centers of the lenses closer together than the edges, which bend light outward.

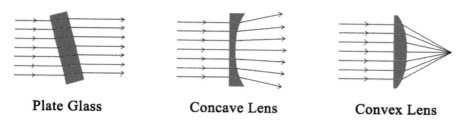

Plate Glass   **Concave Lens**   **Convex Lens**

FIGURE 1.12
Principles of refraction.

Even without a curved surface, light can be refracted in predictable means even though there is some amount of dispersion in all transparent materials. The first, a principle used in some projectors as well as fiber optics, is known as Total Internal Reflection (TIR). This is a special case of refraction which can have reflective properties. When light travels from a high-index material to a lower-index material, if the angle of incidence is at a critical angle, then refraction is at 90 degrees. If the angle of incidence is greater than the critical angle, light bounces back. This is observed when standing at the edge of a large swimming pool; it is impossible to see the deep end of the pool when it is filled with water, even when the surface is not turbulent.

Another key use of refraction for fiber optics is known as Birefringence. This takes place when light passes through materials with two indices of refraction for the same wavelength of light (usually this must be nearly pure crystals). The material will allow light with the electrical field oscillating in a vertical direction to have a different index of refraction than the same light oscillating in the horizontal direction. This allows for more data to be passed over the same fiber without interference. Fiber optics require laser light, which is a single-color light where the wavelengths line up (known as coherence), keeping them from spreading out.

Perception of Light
All animals are able to perceive some form of light through photoreceptive cells. In the absence of the visible light spectrum, humans cannot see. We may still be able to perceive our surroundings based on our other senses, but our sense of sight requires light to be present and directed to our eyes. While this may seem to be extremely basic, it is important to understand how our eyes collect the visible spectrum and how our brain interprets that information.

Our eyes utilize the same principles of manipulating light which we just discussed. Light enters the eye through the cornea, which is a convex lens containing a transparent liquid. The iris is colored muscles which control the size of the pupil (the black hole in the center), allowing a regulated amount of light to enter the rest of the eye. Light then passes through the lens, which is dynamically shaped by the muscles surrounding it. The bulk of the eye contains a transparent jelly to allow light to pass to the inside wall of the eye, known as the retina.

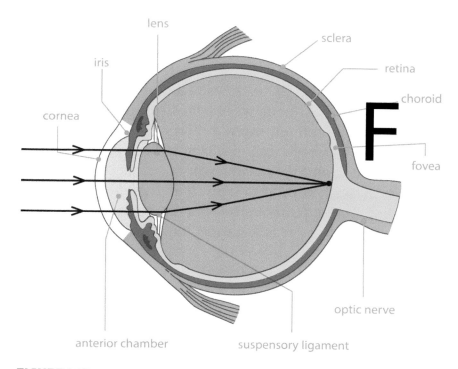

FIGURE 1.13
Diagram of the human eye.

Source: Shutterstock

On the surface of the eye are different photochemical receptors known as rods and cones. Rod cells detect varying levels of light (brightness), while cone cells detect the red, blue, and green wavelengths of light. More specifically, the rod cells are used for low light vision (scotopic) while cone cells are used for bright/daylight vision (photopic), where humans best see color. In the twilight realm of theater, both the rods and the cones are active; this is known as mesopic vision. These cells send signals down the optic nerve to the brain to interpret the information. Some interpretation includes inverting the image observed, as the optics of the eye have already primarily inverted the image.

If we cannot see without light, one of the first questions that might be asked is about the amount of light needed to see. The average consumer will likely think of light in terms of watts. This is due to many years of buying incandescent light bulbs which gave that measurement as the standard. The consumer would know that a certain wattage was necessary to light a given room. As more energy efficient compact fluorescent lamps (CFLs) and light emitting diodes (LEDs) have become more prevalent in stores, their packaging often states the wattage of that fixture, plus the incandescent equivalent. In order to quantify the actual amount of light, scientists developed various means of measurement. The total amount of light given off by a source is known as luminous flux, which is measured in lumens.

Understanding how much light is emitted will help to understand how much can actually be seen. Light radiates out from its source in all directions. Engineers will use various lenses and reflectors to direct light into a desired path. The light will now radiate in a specific beam spread to the display surface. For this, the measurement now requires to know how much light is being emanated and area of the surface illuminated.

In the United States, this is measured in foot-candles, which represent one lumen per square foot. By means of the metric system, it is measured as lux, which is one lumen per square meter. As the area being measured is different, it is good to know that one foot-candle equals 10.76 lux. Thus, the farther an object is away from the source, the more the light spreads, which allows it to cover a greater area, which diminishes the amount of light in any given portion of the overall area. There

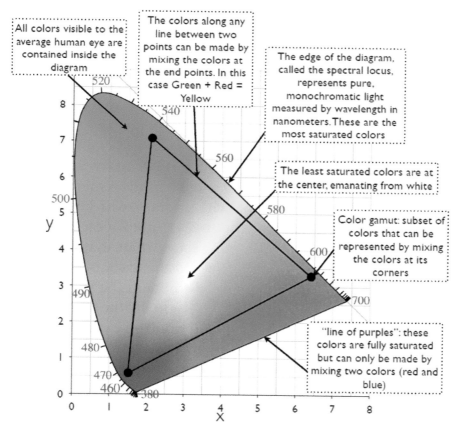

Anatomy of a CIE Chromaticity Diagram

FIGURE 1.14

CIE 1931 chromaticity diagram with representative color rendering area.

Source: Jeff Yurek

are more factors involved, which will be addressed as we discuss the display surface.

How each individual sees light will be a little bit different. While we will discuss the best practices in visual presentation throughout this text, the designer must also realize that every individual will perceive it based on their own eyes. While our eyes are remarkable tools, what we see is subjective. Eyes, similar to our other senses, can be desensitized to a stimulus; this is generally known as fatigue. Looking at a particular color for too long can make us less perceptive to it for a period of time. If you wear blue colored lenses for a long time, get used to how you see the world, then remove those lenses, green and yellow will be particularly vibrant for a time. This is important to note as we get more into the process of calibrating displays as well as the perception of how the audience will perceive the image.

As each of us sees color differently, it is necessary to quantify what we are talking about. The most common method is by utilizing the CIE 1931 chromaticity diagram, which represents the average range of human vision as to limits of each color we see as divided from white. There is some debate that we should only use CIE 1976, but that is beyond the reach of this book. As our brains interpret the selected colors of the visible spectrum, they have to guess at times. This is why the chromaticity diagram varies from the wavelengths on the electromagnetic spectrum. You will notice that there is a triangle within the total area. This represents what a display or a screen can transmit, illustrating that it may never match real life. This is constantly being improved and the triangle continues to expand. This will come into play more as the designer who gets to select equipment can take greater control over the finalized design.

CHAPTER 2

Design Elements

How do you know what you want, until you get what you
want, and see if you like it?

~Stephen Sondheim, *Into the Woods*

While *Into the Woods* is not about new media design, there
can be many parallels to the design question. For instance, the
script is a combination of fairy tales brought together to tell a
story. The media designer will be one of the creators to help
tell a story. While the above quote may ring true about many
things in life, it is most assuredly true for those attempting
video for live performance the first time. It may take many
different productions before a designer will be able to accurately conceptualize how media will look before getting into
the space. Even when he or she has that experience, conveying
it will still be challenging. The director will certainly have a
vision, but whether that aligns with what can be created will
be determined by the media design team. To start, let us look
at that team who will be bringing about the vision.

DESIGN TEAM

There are a variety of departments with which the media design
team will collaborate. For most productions, there is a certain
commonality in the design team in the roles and duties each

individual is taken to accomplish. As with all productions, these may be combined or spread out depending on need and type of production. No matter how the team is created, there are certain job functions which are present in each design.

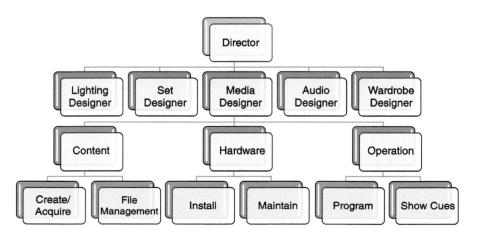

FIGURE 2.1
Media design hierarchy.

Designer

As with other departments, at the top of the team will always be a designer. This person will actively participate in the discussion of the integration of the various elements, their effects, the aesthetics to be created, and the budget considerations. The director may have decided to include video elements from the start and the media designer will be hired at the very beginning, which may lend itself to better integration into the production overall. However, this element of the production may come in after other elements are already underway, possibly at the last possible moment. If the media designer comes in late to the production, the only additional challenge will be working within the umbrella of other design elements underway. In either case, communication between other departments will be critical to success.

There are different approaches that the designer may employ. The first approach is simply equipment based, or working within a set scope of equipment that is available at hand. This may be the most common in a repertory or community theater that has acquired various pieces of equipment over time and may not have the ability to supplement additional elements. The equipment may be of various ages or possibly purchased as one complete system. This does not mean that this will automatically lead to a perfect or a poor design, but instead gives the designer a set of parameters that must be worked within.

Next, there is the budgetary based design, which equipment will need to be acquired through rental or purchase to fit within a specific budget. This will be the most common with large-scale shows and tours. It will give the designer greater flexibility by allowing them to choose best how to realize his or her vision. It is unlikely that the designer will need to worry about elements missing which would compromise the design.

Finally, there is the pure concept based design, where the visual elements will likely be highlighted in the production and any element needed to realize that concept will be able to be obtained or created. This design style is not necessarily bound by what is currently available to all designers. Writing a custom program or having a manufacturer alter existing equipment may be required; these are steps that have been taken in the past by designers to achieve this concept. This will likely help the production stand out but may come at a heavy financial expense or could increase the amount of time of pre-production.

The designer will be involved with the production meetings to discuss the integration of the design into a production with other show elements and will be able to describe the aesthetics, the pacing, and the mood, as well as the financial impact on the production. He or she needs to be able to fully envision how the end result will appear. Communication with the director is crucial, as with all designers, to ensure that the design fits within the overall scope of a production. This is where some media designers end up talking themselves out of a job, when they understand that what the director wants can be better served by some other element, including simple tools commonly used by the lighting department.

Visual media can be used extremely effectively or, unfortunately, very poorly. The difference can come down to how well the ideas and needs were communicated between members of the production team. Video, being larger than life, can easily upstage the rest of the performance.

Content Creator

The designer may or may not be the one who creates the actual content for a production. As productions get larger, there is a likelihood that the designer will not create the content but will have that done by another individual or team. The content creator will acquire all visual elements and prepare them to be used in the media design. This may include still images, video for playback, and video loops, as well as elements to be used with particle generation and interactive media. They will be optimized for the hardware within the design. The designer will have specified the equipment that will be used in the final production so that the content will display properly.

Depending on the complexity of the overall production, the designer may bring in the content team very early on. If the design will have relatively few elements which need to be designed from scratch, it is possible that the content team will not be brought in until shortly before the show is mounted. On some occasions, very complex visuals may take weeks or months to prepare and may need to be delegated to multiple teams.

There are many artists and companies that specialize in the creation of video content. The content may be purchased or commissioned for a particular production. The designer, or possibly a member of the projection design team, may be responsible for creating the content in-house as well. As rendering times can be lengthy, depending on quality and amount of content, good communication between the designer, director, and content creator is essential for keeping a production on schedule. Often the content will be built as elements which can be further manipulated by the presentation equipment, especially when live compositing with media servers. How the content will be used in the actual production can have dramatic effects in how it is created and stored.

Operator and Programmer

Assuming that the production will be utilizing computer elements, such as a media server, the media team will need a programmer and operator. Depending on the duration of a production, the operator and programmer may be the same or different individuals. Even with simple designs, a dedicated operator is preferred to combining the role with a separate department.

The programmer is responsible for inputting the content into digital media players and media servers. He or she will create the look the designer envisions, including the cueing of transitions and effects. If the operator and programmer are not the same individual, then there will need to be clear communication as to how the production will run so that the operator will have the greatest success, including pre-planning for show stops.

The operator should be calm and focused in the production environment, with a complete understanding of the equipment being used. This allows the operator the ability to react to the ever changing environment of live production, especially in the event of equipment failure or dynamic occurrences that may arise, such as delays or changes of show order. It is possible that there will not be any computer elements. The operator could be working with more direct elements such as those used in the broadcast industry. The operator is often much more involved with the designer in this instance as cues will be much more manual and may require a greater skill in operation.

The programmer and operator likely will not come into the production until very close to mounting the show. The programmer may be in contact with the content creation team in order to establish the best format to work with the equipment. This will help to ensure that the media will behave as expected without issue.

Hardware Technician

While this may fall within the realms of the operator and programmer, it is likely that the installation and maintenance will fall to yet another group of specialized technicians. They will be responsible for the infrastructure of signal distribution as well as the display devices. Entertainment can be quite hard on production equipment, which must sometimes operate in harsh environments and often with atmospheric effects that can change the quality of the image. These technicians will provide routine equipment inspections and preventive maintenance and will be able to provide some field repairs. A lot of production equipment is designed to be modular, allowing for simple field service, as opposed to installation equipment, which requires repair in a controlled shop environment.

For long-running production shows, as well as some theatrical environments, the equipment will be semi-permanently installed in the facility. This allows the media team plenty of time to optimize the system. Even when this is not the case, knowledge of the equipment, how it works together, and potential interference is crucial to the installation process. On larger productions, installation may occur while the designer is working with the programmer and content creation team, requiring specific communication in order to keep the design on track.

The designer may approach the hardware team at the beginning for recommendations on equipment to be used. This is the case as the designer will be the one who is working directly with the director on the budget and will need this information to realize the design. Knowledge of the equipment to be used will be essential to the content creation team as well as the programmer.

DESIGN PROCESS

As with any element of the production, the media designer will create a style based on the production as a whole. How he or she does so is generally based on one of two main principles, as previously mentioned. In most productions the designer will work under the process of having the design idea and obtaining the equipment necessary to fulfill that idea, or they will be working under the constraints of a budget and using equipment that is available on hand. In rare instances, the designer will have completely free rein and have the artistic vision that will be fulfilled regardless of the budget.

Budget Based Design

Most designers, especially beginning designers, will likely fall into this design philosophy. It cannot be repeated enough: adding media design can be an expensive element of a production. Because of this, theater companies and road houses will likely invest in a certain infrastructure to which all designs must conform in some fashion. Some theaters will permanently mount projectors front of house, limiting the designer to front projection from that specific position. Other houses may have a variety of equipment, which gives the designer more freedom, but still constrains him or her to the limitations of equipment available.

On the other hand, some productions will have a budget to rent or purchase the equipment to be used. If a company is considering the investment in having house equipment for the purposes of many shows, they will need to greatly consider a number of elements to allow the greatest amount of flexibility for future productions. Allowing room to expand the system is critical, so that as budget allows, continual improvement is available. The equipment will be discussed in particular throughout this text in order to better understand what is needed to build a system for optimal performance. Companies that regularly produce long-running productions with a lot of media designs will find it in their best interest to purchase equipment and supplement with rentals. Meanwhile, the company that tends to rarely use media may want to consider rental only, even if it greatly increases the cost of a single production.

It should be emphasized that being constrained by the equipment available does not translate to a poor design. Sometimes the simplest solutions can have a great impact. It is possible to make a huge impression with a smaller system based on the audience's perception. Also, the designer should not discount older technology, as a simple slide projector may suffice as part of the design.

Conceptual Based Design

Large-budget productions will often give the designer the flexibility to conceptualize the design and then obtain the hardware and software necessary to complete it. This will often require a larger design team as each portion of the design will take specialized individuals to accomplish the vision. The roles listed above will be filled by several individuals with fewer overlaps. The designer may work with previously installed equipment, but likely will be working with a rental house to build the system required for the production or purchase all of it for a permanent production. In addition, especially with interactive elements, the designer may employ those outside of the entertainment industry to help fulfill the vision. There may be a greater amount of time needed to be dedicated to research and development of those outside elements. Certain budgetary considerations will always be present, but the main difference is that the designer will have greater freedom to create something that may not have been seen before.

COLLABORATION

As previously mentioned, media design may be the one element that requires the greatest amount of collaboration with other parts of the production. Of course, to have any successful production, there is the requirement that all departments work together. This part of the production has several elements that can have a great impact on whether or not it achieves its goal. The success can be jeopardized at any point, by any department. Much of this communication will take place during the planning stages of the production; however, many elements will be too difficult to predict until actual installation of the production.

Carpentry

As the department in charge of scenery, carpentry will generally oversee the projection surfaces as well as the scenic elements which may contain monitors or LED panels. They will need to understand the specific needs of a good display (how scenery is surfaced, including paint) and how to protect video surfaces (screens) if they are used. As rigging may be a part of carpentry, they may also need to be consulted for mounting of projectors,

LED walls, and any other elements used in the design. As is critical with lighting designers, the media designer will need to know specifics of the plan and elevation of the set pieces as a means to have optimum angle and distance when using projection.

Lighting

The most obvious conflict with the lighting department is how much direct or ambient light will fall on the display surface. It does not take much to compromise the image. The media designer and lighting designer will need to work closely together to ensure that there is enough light on the set and performers, but not so much that it competes with projection. This may cause issues on the angle of the lighting instrument, as light reflected off of surfaces, not always direct light, will cause the problem. If the design and budget allows, this can be minimized or eliminated through the use of LED walls. In that case, the designers will need to know how the emissive display will affect the backlighting of the performers.

The lighting department will be responsible for providing power to the video system. Electronic interference can be problematic, as can the potential for ground loops in an analog system, so knowing the source and path of power is essential. In addition, if video playback is providing an audio feed, clean power is necessary as well to make sure no noise is introduced into their system. The design team must understand all of their power needs in order to effectively communicate them with the electrics department, such as inrush as compared to operating power.

Audio

Audio and video are commonly associated in the community at large and are often referred to as a single audio visual department, primarily due to an industry which defines itself in this manner. Prior to the modern surge of video for live performance, the audio department handled many video elements. In theater, they have been in charge of the closed circuit television used for monitoring activities on stage by stage management and musicians needing to see the conductor. Some of the video and audio use similar co-axial cables for distribution, though resistance in the cables is different. In addition, audio signals can fall prey to the same kinds of interference that video signals can, so by keeping them together it is easier to keep them protected. Finally, audio is often tied directly to video in terms of image magnification (IMAG) and coordination of visual and audio effects, as well as standard playback of cinema. The audience will often be able to perceive a slight delay between audio and visual elements.

Artistic

Directors, producers, and others within the artistic staff will have their own vision of the media design. They may not understand everything that brings the artistic vision to fruition and may make demands that are difficult, if not impossible, to achieve due to those pesky laws of physics. The producers will ultimately have a say on the budget, which may put constraints or new challenges on the projection team.

A video system can add considerable costs to a production, especially one with an extended run. Rental may be ideal for a short run, but in just a couple of months, rental costs can exceed the purchase price of much of the gear. On the other hand, a production company that chooses to purchase their equipment can quickly become constrained by their choices as they are locked into the specifications. There is always some flexibility in a system, but the amount available increases with the price point. A risk is also present that the equipment purchased may be at the end of a production run, limiting its future serviceability, or it may be incompatible with newer gear that is acquired or rented later.

Other challenges that may surface are misconceptions about the ability of the design and the lack of properly trained staff to use the equipment. Along with the rise of video systems in the theatrical market, many advances have been made in the home entertainment sector. This is good for lower budget productions, but it can be difficult for designers to communicate some of the very distinct differences between consumer and professional goods.

With a little bit of knowledge about home systems by the director, greater challenges can arise in the professional sector through the false assumption that all elements are always plug-and-play; professional equipment allows much more flexibility, which requires more knowledge in setup. Another common myth is that changing the imagery is simple. While this can be the case with proper preparation, depending on the quality of the media, it could take days to render changes.

The design team may also run into problems finding adequately trained staff. Those who know the equipment and content are often trained in the broadcast or convention industry and may not have experience in theatrical settings. More often, there are those in theater who have an extremely steep learning curve to learn to work with the great amount of technology at their disposal and how to make it work effectively. Those who are highly qualified find that freelancing is often more lucrative than working with a smaller production company or on a permanent production. Several universities are currently taking on the challenge to correct this discrepancy.

FUNCTIONS OF DESIGN

While there are many elements to the design process, including the method of design, exploring the functions can be critical in learning how to build the entire system. Some designs will have a solitary function; however, most designs will contain multiple functions, which add complexity. Obviously, there will be variations that do not tend to fit exactly into any one function, either. This is not a right or wrong type of thing, but just another tool to make the design better. For instance, the designer may choose to mix in specific equipment to handle individual parts of the design instead of trying to have one all-encompassing piece. On the other hand, if separate equipment is not available, concessions may be made to serve multiple functions with a single display.

Informative

The first function is simply to provide information. There are many times in a script where a time and place are very specific and need to be disseminated. When setting the stage that may not instantly be understood by the audience, putting text in an area that is visible can help move the production along quite well. Outside of traditional theater productions, there is also a need to convey information to the audience, and legibility is of a great concern.

FIGURE 2.2

Example of informative function—*Les Misérables.*

Source: Broadway Media Distribution, Inc.

As seen in Figure 2.2, for the musical *Les Misérables*, the city and date are displayed before certain scenes to establish an understanding of the progression of the story. On the other hand, when doing a foreign language production, such as an opera, there may be the desire to add a subtitled translation to the set in some productions. In house of worship productions, this is often used to provide lyrics to the congregation. These could be realized through various methods. In the latter case, a simple screen and projector will often suffice as full phrases of music. For the purpose of subtitles, the audience will want to not avert their eyes far from the action. So, full screen dialogue will not be ideal. If using a projector in this instance, much of the image will be wasted to black space, only using a small portion for the actual characters. This may not be problematic if the designer is also using the same projector for other purposes in the production, but could choose to use something like dedicated LED panels instead.

Legibility of text can be of great concern. The use of very stylized fonts need to be scrutinized depending on the complexity of what is being said. For something like the subtext in an opera or lyrics in the house of worship, a very simple font should be used so that the audience may quickly read the information. If the audience is spending too much time discerning text, they will be missing out on critical elements of the performance. However, should the information be brief, such as the aforementioned city and date in *Les Misérables*, a more stylized font can be used, as well as other elements behind the text, as it does not compete with the rest of the production.

Environmental

Creating scenic elements is one of the original and longest lasting uses for projected media, and likely what is most preferred to add to a production. Adding a projected backdrop is currently a very desirable element to many theater companies

FIGURE 2.3
Example of scenic function—*A Gentleman's Guide to Love and Murder.*

Source: Aaron Rhyne

41

who may not have the budget for scenic painters, especially when there is a need to create multiple drops. There is a misconception that this will always be cheaper and easier. There will be some financial benefits at some point, but the initial investment may be shocking. Some of the advantages include the ability to alter the backdrop live, creating a more cinematic feel. An added benefit is that various scenic elements can be created on almost any surface. While companies may have multiple drops, the ability to change the look of a multi-surface scenic element is the stronghold of projection design, especially when there is the addition of motion to that image, such as water rushing down the side of a set piece.

The scenic function can be further broken down into various subsets. As with a traditional backdrop, it adds a virtual scenery. However, this has the advantage over a painted scenic drop in that it does not need to remain static; it has the ability to change, adding life to the scenery. This exemplifies why many productions want to have media as an integral portion of the show. With the power of modern computers and the flexibility of media programs to form the image to non-standard surfaces, as well as the ever increasing availability of the equipment, this will continue to be a part of the designs.

In addition to setting the scene in a traditional manner from the perspective of the audience, it can also offer an alternate perspective. The content for this may be used in place of other action on stage or in conjunction with other automation. If the content were to show the audience a bird's-eye view of the scene, it would be difficult for the actors to incorporate themselves into the action without the assistance of complicated rigging to compete with gravity. However, if the performer were "walking" along a cliff edge, it would be conceivable for them to scoot along the floor with the audience seeing the perilous "drop" being shown.

The virtual scenery could be somewhat dissociative of the actual location of the character. As a character describes another time or place, the virtual scenery could help to show that in particular, such as floating on the clouds while the character is on drugs. While illustrating the performer's words, this offers a dual representation of the actuality of the dialogue and an expressionistic view of the character's emotional state.

This function of media presentation can suffer the same consequences as a painted backdrop in the sense of perspective. That which looks beautiful on its own can easily destroy the sense of the suspension of disbelief as the actors approach it (as with forced perspective scenery). Scale can be difficult to identify as the designer builds on a relatively small computer monitor: how will the actor look next to that image? However, this may be more easily correctable due to the fluid nature of the media, allowing the designer the ability to adjust as the performer approaches. It does offer the benefit of being the least distractive of all the functions of media, in that it should most easily blend with the rest of the production.

Emotive

Often, media is used to elicit an emotional response. This can be through recognizable objects such as national flags or through culturally known historical videos such as those depicting Nazi Germany, but can also exist in unrecognizable patterns. The purpose of this function is that the designer can rapidly advance an emotional feeling from the audience by working through preconditioned responses. This form of commentary tends to utilize very large images, incorporating much of the audience's view. It appears to dwarf much of the other action. As with many other media, there is a fine line between success and upstaging the rest of the performance.

This can be used as a melodramatic effect, the same way a musical score has been found to enhance emotional response in television and film productions. Affective media does not

FIGURE 2.4
Example of emotive function—The Who's *Tommy*.

Source: Peter Cunningham

exist directly in the character's world. It is a relationship to the emotions of the character. A designer has a few ways of eliciting this effect.

An emotive function could be seen as a synesthetic response to the action on stage. Synesthesia is a neurological/physiological condition where human senses can react to a different sense's input. Thus colors could be seen in response to an audio stimuli. Even though the character may not suffer from this condition, a visual designer could easily use this as a medium for helping to stimulate the audience's emotional response.

The media can offer a subjective perspective by illustrating the thoughts and dreams of one or more of the characters onstage. This will heighten the audience perspective of the emotions felt by the characters. The designer may choose to incorporate real-time interactive elements that the performer can utilize as he or she feeds off the emotions of the audience. In any case, this has the ability to offer the designer a lot of creative input, though caution should be used to prevent distracting the audience.

Special Effect

The special effect may be the most subtle of the design functions, with the exception of something such as Pepper's Ghost. It will often be used in conjunction with other production elements. Designers will often use media when there may be a need to create what might normally be a physical special effect in a production, but due to considerations such as budget, experience, or safety, an effect created through video may be more desirable. This might include making a fire in a fireplace or, as a much safer way of displaying explosions, including fireworks. It could also be used as a method of accentuating something physical, such as creating a hail of arrows when only

45

FIGURE 2.5

Example of special effect function—*A Christmas Carol.*

Source: Jon Hyers, Outrageous Media

a few physical arrows could be fired or the addition of flowing lava to a volcanic set piece. Something which may need to be temporary, such as a splatter on a wall, could be projected and easily removed. However, the effect can also have a practical purpose. Many times a director will have a television facing upstage with only a flickering lighting effect to represent a working unit, but there could be a need for it to actually work.

When media is used as a special effect, it rarely will be using a traditional surface. Often, this is where projected media is used to help create an ethereal effect. Pepper's Ghost will rely on a reflective yet transparent surface (as seen in Figure 2.5 with the ghost of Jacob Marley). Other times, other semi-transparent surfaces such as theatrical smoke or scrim will be used. These non-traditional surfaces allow for the audience to perceive the projected media differently than the same material would appear on a regular screen.

In addition to accentuating the set and performance area, special effects have also been used to project on a performer's face or wardrobe. This will either take very precise rehearsal with the video to make it work or else it will take a very complex system to allow it to react to the performer. In any case, this should help to illustrate that media can be used in many other ways.

Many of these techniques will fall into the category of augmented reality. This is where the real world is altered through the use of media. In rare cases, the audience could use a head-mounted display where a live image is shown with the addition of media.

Textural
Unlike the scenic design that provides a recognizable atmosphere, a textural design is aesthetic. Though not often used in theater, it is an important tool for various live performances.

FIGURE 2.6
Example of textural function—The Beatles *LOVE.*

Source: Tomas Muscionico

Often these will be abstract or geometrical shapes that are seen as visuals along with music, generally seen at concerts and raves. This type of imagery is also often used at corporate conventions to help give life to otherwise sterile presentations.

Unlike the emotive function, this type of media is not created to elicit emotions, though it can add quite a bit of excitement. Similar to scenic and emotive functions, the textural function is often larger than the performers and as such has the risk of distracting from them. There is not the risk of overpowering a performer at music performances where the textural media is the visual center of the performance.

Live and Interactive

As a more specialized field of design, this function relies on the precise nature of the human element. Even if there is nothing pre-recorded, it often requires a lot of preparatory work. In corporate presentations and music concerts, this is most evident through a technique known as image magnification, or IMAG. In this process, one or more cameras will be trained on the subject and relayed to a large display in order to allow audience members further from the stage to see the presenter or other performer. In a theatrical performance, additional layers of media could be present with the IMAG.

FIGURE 2.7
Example of IMAG—*Zarkana*.

Source: Matt Beard

With a greater amount of computer processing, this function is gaining additional popularity through the use of the performer manipulating images through motion capture and other interactive elements. This can be accomplished through many different technologies. Motion capture is the process of using a camera to view the movement of an object in order to provide the data for some other purpose. This can be creating an object through particle generation or the distortion of an image. To aid the camera, sometimes tracking objects are added to the target, allowing for more precise data. Other means of tracking motion, though in a more two-dimensional sense, is through the use of inductive, capacitive, or pressure sensitive surfaces, as well as encoder data from automated pieces. Capturing the motion of a performer can easily be turned into virtual puppetry. This is where not only does the camera see the performer, but a computer will track the movement of the performer and create a different character.

FIGURE 2.8
Example of interactive—*KÀ*.

Source: Eric Jamison

Components of Design

Finally, there are five main pieces to the video system puzzle. Each of these pieces may be further divided into individual components depending on a particular system design. In addition, there will be many variations based on the design requirements, so all systems will have some similarities; some may also not combine all of the elements. The three fundamental pieces will be the source, the display, and the distribution of media information between them. These three will be a part of almost every design. For more complex systems, there will be a system of control and a network of communications. These will be discussed separately as well, as their relationships can be less than obvious. To see sample systems, make sure to check out Appendix A.

CHAPTER 3

Source Material

The first thing to consider in any design is what the audience will ultimately see. The source material to be presented is known as content. Later on we will refer to the source as the technology which contains the content and method of playback. Content can either be created during the production process, so it is simply played back during a show, or it can be specific variables within a program which allow it to be created live. Not every designer will have the ability to create the content necessary for a production, just as not every sound designer is a composer or creates their own effects. Most media designers will turn to others for at least some portion of their content.

STOCK CONTENT

There are many companies who provide content to be used in part or as a whole for media designers for a fee. Some produce the content themselves while others are host sites that jury content from independent artists. The media will range from digital photography to computer generated still images, vectors to be used in conjunction with other images, recorded animation, time-lapse footage, and even a variety of videos which loop seamlessly. All of the media will be formatted in such a way that it is ready to use on its own as well as edited.

Stock content may be packaged with a digital device that is rented or purchased. This is often the case with media servers used by digital lighting designers. If the device is rented, the rental company should have reset the equipment to factory settings when it was returned, which would erase all content that was not originally packaged with the system, as the next designer to use the equipment will likely not know what should be there or not. The rights to the stock content on the server were obtained by that manufacturer and they will have protections to prevent it from being misused, such as preventing it from being removed from the server. Before using any material that has not been created by the designer, he or she must understand the legality of doing so.

Copyright

Laws are in place to protect intellectual property. This is the type of property that is, on its own, intangible. These laws protect authors, artists, and composers with the exclusive right to make copies, distribute, or otherwise grant the use of their work. The laws, at least in the United States, grant the exclusive right to the creator for his or her lifetime, and, up to 50 years after their death, to their beneficiaries. What this means to the media designer is that if the content is not created specifically by the designer, permission must be obtained to use the media. This means that even if media is found in a publicly available forum, such as a library, or especially the internet, it does not mean that the media is free to be used.

Many artists will ensure that their copyright is protected by putting various digital protections on their work to prevent copying, or else have a watermark present until purchase. Unless it is specifically stated that the content is not protected under copyright, it should be assumed that it is. In fact, U.S. copyright protection is implied for all creative work unless it is specifically published that it is freely available. Artists can register their work to help prove that they rightfully own the work. As an alternative to filing for an official copyright on a work, digital designs can be put onto a physical storage medium, such as files burned to disk and mailed to yourself. The unopened package with the postmark has stood up in court in the past. This does require that you still have a method of burning a disk, which is becoming less common.

The copyright laws were established to help protect a person's creation. For many artists, these creative efforts are their livelihood. The desire to avoid paying for content can often be a temptation for a designer who is working for a not-for-profit company or event that has little to no budget for media. Even if the media designer has chosen to work for free, this does not mean that the original artist has done the same.

FIGURE 3.1
Copyright, Creative Commons, and Public Domain.

Content is not protected internationally, as U.S. law is only binding in the United States and its territories. This means that once the artist's work is taken outside of the area in which copyright law can protect it, the designer must either apply for protection from other countries or attempt to have it protected under the international treaty known as the Berne Convention for the Protection of Literary and Artistic Works. However, it comes to the rights holder to attempt to recover compensation in whichever country the offense took place. This is easier

53

for large companies than sole proprietorships, which most designers fall under.

An American nonprofit organization added to this, creating a designation of Creative Commons. So, no longer is a work "all rights reserved", but it may be deemed "some rights reserved" or may allow use to the public provided that attribution is made. The intent of this type of protection was to expand creativity by allowing others to legally build upon works of others. However, since the copyright office does not keep a database of all works, it does not absolutely absolve the work of copyright protection, as the work may be negligently uploaded.

Royalty or Royalty Free

As mentioned, there are many companies who make content available to media designers. On rare occasions, the site will provide content free of charge with limited conditions such as only being used on not-for-profit productions and including a mention in the design credits. More often, the site will allow use for a fee. There are two methods for these fees to be processed: either by royalty or royalty free.

Media distributed under a royalty contract means that a fee will be paid for every use of the media. What this means for the media designer is that the media will cost a certain amount for every performance, but not for rehearsals. Media designed under a royalty contract will likely be a complete work designed for a specific production and may have restrictions on how it may be presented.

On the other hand, the designer will find much more flexibility by obtaining rights through royalty free media. This is a type of agreement where rights to the content are purchased to be used without paying a royalty per performance. There are a variety of contract terms for how royalty free media can be used. The media designer must abide by their contracts which allow the use of the intellectual property. Some companies will allow the designer to use the content in perpetuity, for as many productions as they wish, so long as they do not distribute the content themselves. Other companies will put restrictions such as a limitation on the number of commercial uses. Limited use will help keep content fresh and free from overuse. Some licenses will grant use only if the content is altered in some way, such as being combined with other content. Make sure to read the fine print to avoid any legal issues.

Public Domain

Content which was created after January 1, 1978, will be protected under the U.S. copyright for 50 years after the death of the artist. After that point, the copyright is released to the public domain. There may be other means by which a work of art will have the status of being in the public domain. What this means to the media designer is that the original work does not have the protection of a copyright, but belongs to the public. This means that the designer does not have to pay a royalty to use the material, but there could be a fee associated with obtaining the content from a provider. The Creative Commons organization established a mark similar to the copyright mark (a letter c in a circle) by altering it with a strikethrough. This may be present in some works to allow the designer to know for sure that the work is not protected by a copyright. All works that have not been specifically given over to the public domain or fallen out of copyright protection should be assumed to still be protected. In the digital age, it is both easy to find and utilize work from the public domain and difficult to know if it is truly available.

Fair Use

There is a provision within the copyright law known as fair use. This is a sticky area and could be beneficial to a designer, but easily can become a legal nightmare. There are a lot of assumptions that are passed around. The description here should hopefully aid in clarifying the provision, but is not legally binding. When in doubt, seek legal counsel.

Fair use generally falls to documentary films, news reports, or scholarly works, but it may include in some specific instances selected works of fiction. The material might be used in cases of political critique, such as elements of popular culture in order to illustrate an issue in a debate. It might be used as an instance to show historical context. This is brought up as this type of material may be crucial to a design using the emotive function.

Generally, there are four points which should be considered as to whether the use might fall within the U.S. copyright clause on fair use. These include: what is the intended purpose for how the material will be used; what is the nature of the original work; how much of the work is to be used and how central it is to your use; and will your use have an economic impact on the original material. These questions may be difficult to answer, as the means of use in a live theatrical method is often greatly different from the intended purpose of sole viewership.

File Sharing Websites

Digital rights management (DRM) is a method that Hollywood studios and others have used to help prevent fraudulent copying and sharing of movies and other digital entertainment. One of the main reasons that digital encryption methods were implemented was due to the number of file sharing websites. There was a backlash against sites which were allowing copyright to be bypassed by distribution outside of the rightful owner.

File sharing is not in and of itself illegal. There are many websites that will aid the designer and others in the production team to collaborate on a project without always meeting in person. The peer-to-peer architecture allowed many in the past to share digital copies of music and videos. The most popular architecture is still BitTorrent. Many file sharing sites which broach illegal activity have been shut down through various court orders, mainly due to breach of copyrights. The designer should make sure to utilize trusted sites and obtain content from known sources. It is best to consider that you cannot obtain content for free unless you see the explicit release of copyright on the site.

As just mentioned, file sharing websites can be a wonderful tool during the collaboration process. Beyond the peer-to-peer sharing, where the user allows another to access content from their own computer, there are other methods of sharing. Starting around 1985, file transfer protocol (FTP) sites allowed companies to share content with clients, but this can be extremely slow with the large files currently used. Now, cloud storage has become a popular method of sharing. This allows users to upload their content to a third party storage system and allowing others permission to access that information. Some sites allow continued storage while others will have expiring storage, where the content must be downloaded within a timeframe before it is deleted. There are many companies who may be concerned with the security of open source cloud storage as there have been some highly publicized security breaches of some of these systems. There are software systems which will offer greater security, but the necessity and cost may prevent these from being an option for the casual designer.

CUSTOM CONTENT

As companies progress in the complexities of production, they will likely choose to avoid stock content, with the idea that it may not represent their vision or identity. Also, a newer company may not be able to have the budget to purchase or lease content. In this case the designer will need to create all of the content needed and put it together into a usable product. If he or she does not have the skill or equipment to do so, there are a variety of companies that specialize in the creation of video content, if the budget allows. Also, bringing in a content specialist as part of the design team is common in larger productions.

Just as new designers may not know where to start with creating a projection system, they may have never created content. This topic can be discussed in volumes on exactly how to obtain original material, especially in relation to how it fits with the rest of the performance. Unfortunately, there is no way to cover the dramaturgical expectations here. Instead, this section will cover how to use base materials to create something new that will be optimized for presentation.

Non-Linear Editor

As digital media has developed over the years, personal computers often have included at least a basic video editor packaged in the operating system (OS). These programs are very rudimentary non-linear editors. Essentially, a linear editor would be along the lines of how analog editing took place, splicing together film or tape stock. With the analog material, the original material must be destroyed to create the new product. That is not the case with digital media. With a non-linear editing system, there is some similarity to working with a linear editor in that media may be split and combined. However, the original material is not altered when being used in the non-linear editor.

The non-linear editor will allow the creation of entirely new works out of existing works or allow the designer to recode existing content to a new form so that all media matches. A still image can be given movement and dimensionality. A video

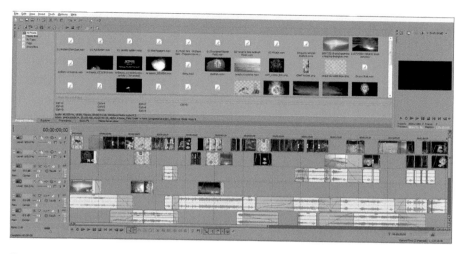

FIGURE 3.2
A non-linear editor workspace.

can be sped up or slowed down and even reversed, changing how it would have been originally perceived. Depending on the production, the editor may include audio in the video so that when show time comes, timing will be less of an issue.

In the creation of new media, a lot depends on the complexity of the editing program. Generally speaking, the more expensive the program, the more options the designer has in creating and manipulating material. On the other hand, those who are relatively new to designing content should probably avoid the high-end professional programs and instead look at high-end consumer grade programs. The difference comes in how the final product is rendered. With the high-end consumer grade programs, there will be limited choices in how the final project is rendered, based on common factors. If the wrong settings are chosen for what can be played on the display, then all the effort in creation will be lost.

Composition

The way that the final product is rendered will have a lot to do with the intent for how it will be displayed. The production begins with the idea of what content is to be displayed, but the goal of the designer is how it will appear to the audience. As part of the workflow, the designer will have to understand the entire process. Creating a composition without knowing how it will be presented may lead to poor performance. You should never count on happy accidents.

The render from the non-linear editor may not appear pretty on the computer in which it is being created as long as it works as the final product. This was evident in old film stock when a 35mm film was to be used with an anamorphic lens. If you were looking at the film stock or a projection with a standard lens, everything would have appeared tall and skinny. The producer would have known that some theaters would have a wide screen and the appropriate projection equipment and thus produced the film stock in that manner. The same could be said for a digital designer; if he or she knows that the final presentation will not be on axis, the content may be created to have keystone correction built in. The more advanced designs may include splitting the image to be blended later or recombined on a three-dimensional (3D) object.

FILE SIZE/COMPRESSION

Imagine analog film if you can. Film stock came in a variety of sizes including 8mm, 16mm, 35mm, and 70mm. Those were physically different sized mediums. In addition, depending on the quality of the film stock, it also had varying thickness. The length of a film clip and the type of film stock used determined the physical space required to store it. Although digital media does not have a physical space correlation, there are many factors that cause it to vary in size. Some of these factors will include resolution, color space, frame rate, and whether it is interlaced or progressive footage. With physical media, if designers were concerned with the physical amount of storage space, they would be relegated to choosing a different film stock, which could change the quality of the finished work.

When using digital media, the choice is the method of compressing the content. This process reduces the data in a signal by eliminating redundant information. This can be described either as lossless or "lossy" compression. The difference in bandwidth reduction will vary greatly depending on the type of compression used.

When we consider a lossless compression, there is a complete restoration of the original data that was in the original image. Lossless images will not be as small of a file when there is a lot of changing data. However, with large areas that do not change from image to image, such as a solid color background, the file will not be as big. Lossless compression is more suited for computer graphics which have very defined color and brightness information. It is most often used for archiving video or for the raw content during the editing process.

Lossy compression is much more of an approximation of the original image. As it is likely that data from pixel to pixel will change more rapidly from footage shot on a camera, lossless compression is not ideal. Thus, by using a less exact method of compression, the image will have a loss of some of the data. As the human eye is most perceptive to changes in brightness, the parts of the compression scheme that deal with brightness will be much more accurate than components which we perceive less. We are also sensitive to motion, so elements that deal with a lot of motion will be compressed less than those that do not. This would be represented in large changes between frames. There are a variety of methods within these two general frameworks. The method of compressing and decompressing the data is known as a codec.

CODECS

A digital video image is similar to that of film in that it is representing one complete picture after another in order to represent movement. The image will change a specified number of times per second, which is known as frame rate. Data is reduced by measuring and registering the redundancies in the image. This can be within a frame (intraframe) or between frames (interframe). Methods such as these are known as sampling.

In intraframe compression, the technique is often known as sub-sampling. There are different means of doing this, either through only looking at alternating pixels or through reducing data collected per pixel (quantization). This means that each frame of the video will have loss and will have poorer representations for general playback, but may not show much difference when scrubbing during playback.

For interframe compression, the codec will be looking at the changing and unchanging portions of successive frames. This way simple changes may be stored as commands for things such as repeated information or simple changes. The data for commands is smaller than that for the original data. There are difference coding, block-based difference coding, and block-based motion compensation, which allows for differences between frames. Each of these compares some difference between frames in order to send commands as opposed to data. Further refinement can come as it compares more frames, such as also comparing the preceding frame, in finding the differences.

There are a variety of different codecs that all have their advantages and disadvantages. Generally speaking, the designer will need to familiarize him/herself with a number of them in order to use them effectively. There will be limitations such as the playback system and accuracy of rendering the image, as well as how it might be manipulated in a live environment. Many of these decisions will be made from a purely subjective standpoint, i.e. what has worked best for you in the past. Some of them will be given as a set limitation by the operator (they know what their system can handle). Depending on the amount of time and storage available, the designer may choose to render the best lossless compression and then convert or re-render the content once on site with the show equipment. In the end, the codec choice will be the one that works best in the relationship between several factors, including the drive access speed, the available RAM (including the video RAM), the speed of the CPU, and the processor cache size. The cache size is of great importance, especially for interframe compression.

Codecs are constantly being improved and new ones are being developed. New displays have much higher resolution, plus they have a greater amount of color information, all of which requires a greater ability to handle the data. This requires new algorithms to be created to handle the greater amount of information to manage file size and the speed of decompression. This can be challenging to designers who are unfamiliar, as legacy equipment often will need to be supported and thus legacy codecs are still available for use in various editing programs that do not serve modern equipment well. In addition, some equipment will have proprietary codecs which can either allow video to best function on their hardware or ensure the security of the video loaded onto it.

63

Digital video stored on or accessed by a computer requires a specific file format. As already mentioned, various forms of compression are used to reduce file size. However, in order to store and transport that file, a container is required. Consider the example of going to a drive-up teller at the bank. You may place your deposit slip and money to be deposited into an envelope (similar to bundling the digital data), but you will be required to put that in a container specifically designed for the pneumatic tube system to send the deposit to the teller. Different containers have been designed to best transport various codecs and these will be shown as the file extension on the video file. Thus, when you glance at a file on your hard drive, you will see the file extension as a suffix to the file name, but you will only be able to infer which codec is used. In addition, the container will store the metadata about the file (the deposit slip) which is additional information about the file itself.

ALPHA CHANNEL/MATTE

Often times there is the desire to mix two different video elements, such as adding a comet to the night sky. One way this is done is kind of like playing with paper dolls. The background will be a layer of video, the comet will be an addition to that layer. Instead of laying an entirely new page of paper that happens to have a comet on it, which would obstruct the entire background, the alpha channel acts like a cutout, allowing just the image of the comet to be seen. The total image component providing the image transparency is the image plane.

The alpha channel specifies the alpha value for each color pixel. Alpha values can be stored in additional bit planes of frame buffer memory. So, a 32-bit frame will have eight bits of each color (red, green, and blue), plus an 8-bit alpha channel (instead of luminance). The result is that the alpha number associated with the alpha channel is greater than where that layer is not appearing, allowing the mixing program to show only the color information of the object, not blending with the colors of the lower layer. Not every program will handle this information, nor does every codec or picture file. In some cases, the alpha channel will appear as a solid white or black background, which will of course obscure the other layer.

FIGURE 3.3
Use of alpha matte.

Similar to the alpha channel is the alpha matte. Again, this is to aid in blending two different picture elements. The alpha matte is used most often in instances where there is not an alpha channel present. So, instead of having a blank channel, the matte works with the luminance value. Most often the alpha matte will be entirely black and white. This acts like a stencil where the black areas block a particular layer while the white areas allow another area to be seen. These can either be static images (like the stencil) or they can be manipulated to work with a video element that, when used in combination, works just like the alpha channel in the compositing environment.

STORAGE AND TRANSPORT

Even with analog technology, there were differences in how information was stored, as was seen between Beta and VHS cassettes. Digital storage has changed over time as well. Optical disk and digital tape stock are almost never used anymore, but they do relate to some of the original digital compression methods such as DVC and MPEG-2. These were used to optimize the storage and transport of NTSC quality video. One of the main reasons that these are less in favor is the increasing quality of the content.

Most digital content will be stored on and accessed from computer hard drives. The drives can be internal to the machine or external. They can be a hard disk drive (HDD), which has an optical platter that spins at different speeds to access the information (generally either 5,400 RPM or 7,200 RPM). These drives are often the least expensive and can have very large capacities for storage. However, they are limited in their speed and are more susceptible to damage from shock. HDDs are good for storing information for archival purposes as long as they are protected from magnetic interference.

Conversely, there is also the Solid State Drive (SSD), which has no moving parts. The access speeds are much greater than in their mechanical counterparts, as SSDs can avoid the seek time that the platter mechanism requires. They come at a substantially greater cost, especially for the decrease in storage space in comparison. These drives also have a lower power usage due to not having moving parts. Internal drives are traditionally connected via cable to the motherboard, though some newer SSDs are connected directly in the PCI (the Peripheral Component Interface bus) slot, which can obtain greater read and write speeds.

There are combination drives which have solid state memory as an addition to a platter drive, but some designers have found that these type of drives wear out in this type of application faster than either of their counterparts. Many have found that they are best for personal computing only, not for performances.

Additionally, multiple drives can be connected through a Redundant Array of Independent Disks (RAID), which can offer greater security of content in addition to greater storage capacity and higher data transfer rates. This can occur in a few different configurations. RAID-0 is a configuration of drives that spreads data across the drives (known as striping). This multiplies disk space as well as data transfer rate. RAID-1 mirrors drives, writing data to multiple drives in a redundant manner, allowing for instant backups. RAID-3, similarly, is used to back up data, but instead of directly mirroring the drives, it uses a technique called parity which places a reference copy of the data on a dedicated disk in case of drive failures or corrupt data. RAID-5 is used by Apple, especially for video editing, and uses a combination of striping and parity. For the truly dedicated, RAID-6 offers the maximum protection, but is unlikely to be used by all but the most crucial of projects. RAIDs can be controlled by software or hardware, with the latter being preferred for speed and not requiring the use of the CPU.

External storage can be any of the previously mentioned drives or it may be on other solid state flash drives in the form of memory cards or "thumb" drives. These solid state media are not all the same. Each varies in size and shape as well as how that media is accessed. Some of the more common forms are Compact Flash, Secure Digital (SD), Secure Digital High Capacity (SDHC), and Secure Digital Extended Capacity (SDXC). A few memory cards will require a specialized drive slot on the computer or require an adapter to use USB (Universal Serial Bus).

Almost all external media will be transported to the computer via a USB port. Ideally, when video is being designed, the hard drive will have little more than the content and associated operating needs on it to reduce collision of data and increase access speeds. It is important to know what the speed of the read/write capacity is per media as well as its transport speed. Solid state capacity will be expressed in megabytes per second (MB/s) while many codecs are expressed in megabits per second (Mb/s). These have a ratio of 8:1 (24 Mb/s is equal to 3 MB/s).

When video is being transported from its storage media, the speed can differ. Take into consideration your external storage or connections of your peripherals. The most common connection is the USB port, when considering access speed. There are different types of USB, which vary both in the shape of the connector and the protocol (as seen in Figure 3.4). USB 2.0, which has been common for quite a few years, can be identified by the four pins used (five in the Mini B) which provide power and data. This is primarily too slow to be used during a performance and should be relegated to storage of smaller files only. USB 3.0 adds an additional two pins of data and has increases in its speed of transport. For this reason, it may be acceptable for use during a performance, depending on the type of drive that the data is coming from, the codec used and

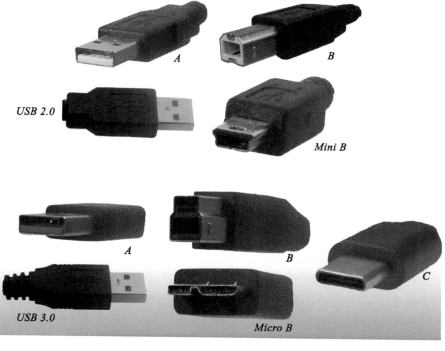

FIGURE 3.4
Select USB identifier.

the size of the file. Some devices have been updated to USB 3.1, which doubles the speed at which it can transfer data. The latest version of USB is known as USB-C. While this is not commonly in use yet, it has the promise of additional speeds which may make it a favorable connection. One advantage to USB-C is the reversible connector, allowing for not needing to know which end is up when adding your connection in the dark spaces of backstage.

In addition, external storage can be connected via PCIe (Peripheral Component Interface express), which is an external means of connecting directly to the motherboard. Speeds obtained are along the lines of the processor and can allow transfer to the Graphics Processing Unit (GPU) directly. Apple

TABLE 3.1 Comparative USB speeds.

USB Host	USB Cable	USB Drive	Expected Speed
3.1	3.0	3.1	10 Gb/s
3.0	3.0	3.0	5 Gb/s
3.0	2.0	2.0	480 Mb/s
2.0	2.0	3.0	480 Mb/s
2.0	2.0	2.0	480 Mb/s

computers developed the Thunderbolt connection for this purpose.

STREAMING VIDEO

As more and more households have become cord-cutters, abandoning traditional cable and satellite television broadcast service in favor of internet based content, consumers are now at least somewhat familiar with streaming video. This allows a remote viewer to access video on demand. To do so, the Real Time Streaming Protocol (RTSP) is used. The RTSP is a network control protocol used to control streaming media servers. It will be used in conjunction with a Transmission Control Protocol (TCP) and a transport protocol. These can be proprietary, though there are some standards, as will be discussed later in Chapter 8.

Streaming video signals will often be beneficial to lighting professionals who are using digital video for lighting purposes. There are also needs for streaming video for multiple location presentations, as well as accessing video which must be stored on a secure server. For whatever reason that streaming media is chosen, there are certain limitations. When streaming media is viewed, the entire video is not generally accessed at once. So, the peripheral accessing the media must have streaming media storage. The storage size depends on the resolution and bit rate. On the server side, bandwidth will vary depending on whether the viewing devices are using a Unicast protocol (similar to home streaming devices that access video on demand) or a Multicast protocol in which the server sends out a single stream that is common to all users (similar to broadcast television). Generally, for live performance, multiple Unicast needs would not be common, so even if the Unicast protocol is used, it would not significantly increase bandwidth requirements. Instead, an IP Multicast is more likely to be used, as performance spaces generally have a private computer network on a local access network.

One benefit is that streaming media can be useful for communication of thumbnails or small video representations, but there are a number of shortfalls for using this in other means during live performance. Reliable protocols, such as TCP, will help to guarantee that the delivery of the media is complete, but it requires that data be complete to proceed. At home, we see this when the signal buffers, allowing for the data to arrive before presenting. This delay is rarely acceptable for viewing by the audience. To minimize the delay, lower resolutions could be used, which can also be unacceptable. Consumer devices will often do this automatically, which can result in a less defined image with multiple artifacts.

RESOLUTION

When we speak of digital displays, one commonly described element is the resolution. Resolution most often refers to the number of picture elements (pixels) present, but can also refer to the amount of color information present. The resolution of a display or video file (still or sequential image) will be described by the number of pixels (width of image) by the number of lines of pixels (height of image), as all video is inherently two dimensional.

TABLE 3.2 Variety of standardized resolutions.

Aspect ratio	Resolution	Aspect ratio	Resolution	Aspect ratio	Resolution	Aspect ratio	Resolution	Aspect ratio	Resolution
4:3	320x240	5:4	1280x1024	16:9	854x408	16:10	320x200	17:9	2048x1080
	640x480		2560x2048		1024x576		1280x800		4096x2150
	800x600				1280x720		1440x900		
	1024x768				1366x768		1680x1050		
	1280x960				1600x900		1920x1200		
	1400x1050				1920x1080		2560x1600		
	1600x1200				2560x1440				
	2048x1536								

Pixel Density/Raster

Originally, the raster was the resolution of an individual CRT display. As we have expanded our technology to work in conjunction with one another, raster now describes the total viewing resolution. Individual LED panels will have a specific number of pixels per panel. However, they are generally used in tandem with many panels, multiplying the pixels viewed in that display. Similarly, projectors are often used together to form a much larger display than an individual projector could accomplish on its own. So the entirety of the projected image is its raster.

Each display will have what is known as native resolution. This is the raster of the individual display. For the optimum display of content on that display, it should match the native resolution, which presents it at a 1:1 pixel ratio. There are times when this is not possible, which will cause the display to interpret the incoming data and use one of a variety of algorithms to recreate the image within its resolution. Each display will have a set number of resolutions that it can process. In order to communicate this, Extended Display Identification Data (EDID) is

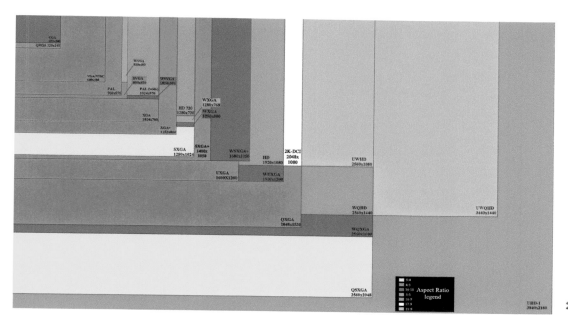

FIGURE 3.5
Comparative resolutions.

used. The standard by which this is accomplished was created by the Video Equipment Standards Association (VESA), which allows the display to communicate its capabilities to the source.

Pixel density is a measurement of the resolution in the electronic image device. This is a comparison of the amount of pixels in a given area. When we look at a computer monitor that is 17″ diagonal as compared to a 42″ flat screen television, which both display a 1920x1080 image, the pixel density of the two images is dramatically different. Knowing the necessary pixel density for a display often depends on the distance to the audience and the content being displayed. Generally, the person sitting in front of a 42″ TV is at a much greater distance than the person sitting at the computer.

When the image does not match the resolution of the display, then there must be some changes made. If the image has less

FIGURE 3.6
Native vs. resized images.

resolution than the native resolution, it can still be displayed pixel for pixel, but it will have blanking around the image. If the user does not want the blanking, the image can fill out the display but there will have to be some information that is interpolated. If you look at the image in Figure 3.6, the image on top was unaltered, but the one on the bottom was resized to match the one on the top. The missing data makes for a poorer image.

Perceived Resolution

As discussed in the Introduction, we are limited by our vision. What we perceive may not always be a direct representation of the quality of the image. Thus, the perceived resolution is actually a combination of the actual resolution (raster), the distance between the observer and the display, and the size of the display (generally measured by the diagonal). This will make a difference, especially when utilizing an LED wall (as discussed in the next chapter).

Display manufacturers are aware of the limitations of human vision and use this when designing a display. Many of us will have experienced at some point a droplet of water landing on our tablet or computer monitor. When this happens, the water magnifies that area of the display, allowing us to see what is providing us the image. Particularly when this happens on a white part of the image, we will be able to see the primary colors of the display separated. Those colors are normally combined by our eyes at the normal viewing distance. The same type of thing will happen with displays for entertainment, which are on a much greater scale as the viewer is also at a much greater distance.

This matter of individual dots combining to create an image originated during the neo-Impressionist movement in the art world during the latter half of the nineteenth century.

Pointillism was a term devised by critics of the works done by artists using this technique. The art was not intended to be viewed up close, but rather at a distance, allowing the natural process of the human eye to blend the colors, as opposed to the palette of the artist prior to applying on the canvas.

As each pixel in a display can only display a single color at a time, the media designer needs to have the right amount of pixels available of the appropriate size to clearly represent their content. Too few pixels can have a variety of effects on the image. As most displays have square pixels, to create a diagonal or curve without the perception of a blocky texture will require a greater density of pixels. Easily recognizable features should also contain more pixels, as associations of the viewer will be more critical as they "know" what it should look like. As greater pixel densities can have a much higher cost involved, finding the right balance between budget and perception will be critical to the designer.

ASPECT RATIO

When the width and height of a display are compared, a simplified ratio of the pixels will be present. For standard definition (SD) video, this used the ratio of 4:3, meaning that for every four pixels across, there were three lines down. Mathematically, this can also be represented as a decimal (1.33:1). Having the mathematical representation allows for easier conversion of comparable displays. Thus, going back to Table 3.2, we can see that the VGA (640x480) is in the same aspect ratio to SXGA+ (1400x1050).

While broadcast television has two aspect ratios, 4:3 for standard definition and 16:9 for high definition (HD), the computer and motion picture industry have additional ratios. When confined to a defined display surface, such as a movie screen or monitor, differences in aspect ratio are generally handled by minimizing the displayed image, so that the entire image is presented but the remainder of the display will be blank video. If an SD image is displayed on an HD display, the center of the display will be filled from top to bottom, but the sides will be blank. This is known as a pillared image. Conversely, if a wide aspect ratio is displayed on a standard definition display, the reduced image will have a blanked image on top and bottom. This is known as letterboxing. This is still present in HD displays when showing cinematic aspect ratios. As SD displays were not always large enough to accommodate the detail of a letterboxed image, consumers often had videos "formatted to fit" their screen. This utilized a technique called pan and scan, essentially omitting the amount of the image which would not fit in that aspect ratio and editing the content so that the relevant image was presented.

Media design does not need to be wholly constrained by aspect ratio other than as a component of the design. Later, as we discuss video walls and blended images, it will be easier to

FIGURE 3.7

Comparison of aspect ratios in a 1080 display.

understand how these various aspect ratios can be utilized to varying degrees or ignored completely. For beginning designs where fewer displays are used, it is more of an issue to maximize the visual image and have it ideally represented.

INTERLACED OR PROGRESSIVE SCAN

When we look at a strip of film, we see a series of consecutive images that, when shown in succession, allow us to perceive movement. Each image in a film is known as a frame. However, when the image is being created by a display device that is not directly projecting the image from a piece of film, then there are two distinct methods to create each frame.

The initial method of creating a frame of information was to combine two separate fields which, when combined by our eye, formed a single frame of information. Due to technology and bandwidth constrictions, this allowed for a greater amount of visual information to be distributed by allowing for

FIGURE 3.8
Interlaced display.

the human perception to fill in the gaps. Even with modern technology, interlaced video will still be used as a method for reducing bandwidth. We see this represented as the number of lines (rows) followed by the letter "i". So, standard definition television is represented as 480i.

To create an interlaced image, the display scans the video across the screen, alternating the odd and even lines. Similar to how English speakers read text, the scanning lines start at the top of the screen; the display scans across, and then moves down. When looking at only one field of the interlaced image, it would appear as if you were looking through Venetian blinds, which prevent you from seeing the complete image. Fast movement is where interlaced footage has its biggest weakness. Between fields, the fast-moving subject can potentially have enough movement that it will look torn, as seen in Figure 3.8. In order to cope with this, interlaced video will sometimes have intentional blurring (anti-aliasing) which reduces interline twitter or other artifacts.

79

Alternately, an image may be progressive. This is often considered to be enhanced video. A progressive image presents a full frame at every scan. This will be represented by a "p" at the end of a line count, such as 720p. As opposed to scanning every other line in two fields as interlaced does, progressive scanning scans all of the lines in sequence for a full frame. This is more common in digital images, while interlaced is more common with analog. As it stores full frames, progressive scanning is ideal for archiving film-based material. Since it displays the full frame at once, there will not be the interline twitter of interlaced footage. Additionally, the designer may capture an individual frame from a progressive scan which can appear as a regular still image.

As older analog displays were designed with interlaced video in mind, nothing had to be processed in order to present it.

On the other hand, digital displays are created with progressive images in mind and thus require an alteration of the interlaced signal. The process for converting interlaced video to progressive is known as deinterlacing. This process can be handled during the creation of content or you can wait and let the front-end processing of the display device handle the conversion. There are a few different methods of doing this.

The first method of deinterlacing is known as field combination. This method simply combines the two fields, as suggested by the name. This can give a look of the image being printed on a basket. However, there are a few methods in which the resultant image can be blended. Additionally, the frame can be made through a process known as field extension deinterlacing. In one version of this method all gaps between scan lines are removed, resulting in a half-sized image. As that changes the aspect ratio, another version will double all of the lines scanned to fill in the gaps. This works better for motion as it will reduce artifacts, but will cause a noticeable issue with still images in that they appear to bob up and down. More advanced methods, known as motion detection deinterlacing, will combine these two methods.

FRAME RATE

The human eye can theoretically distinguish upwards of 1,000 frames every second. What each individual can perceive is considerably less. For several decades, motion pictures were shown at a rate of 24 frames per second (fps). In other words, there were 24 individual pictures presented in sequence for every second which passed. This frequency of sequential images was standardized when sound was introduced to films as an average speed, since most theaters played silent films between 22 and 26 fps. However, this frame rate is the speed in which the frames advanced, even though the projectors would actually show each frame two or three times. The increased rate of showing each image allowed for what is known as flicker fusion. This allows for the persistence of vision to create a smoother image, especially in regard to the mechanics of a projected image.

As video became the standard for home entertainment, new frame rates were established. New frame rates for video were based on the frequency of the power used in the region. For most of the Americas, this was based on a frequency of 60 Hz, and in Europe the frequency is 50 Hz. Due to this, the video frame rate was established at roughly half of these frequencies for data transmission. Further, the NTSC, in order to accommodate for transmission of color and audio subcarriers, established a frame rate of 29.976 (24*1000/1001).

Matching frame rates when displaying media can become challenging when mixing sources of content. Ideally, matching during pre-production will provide the best playback. There are different processes by which this can happen. As film is traditionally 24 fps and video at 30 fps, a process known as telecine is used to match film to video. The method of doing this is known as "pulldown". The 3:2 pulldown is what is used in regions in

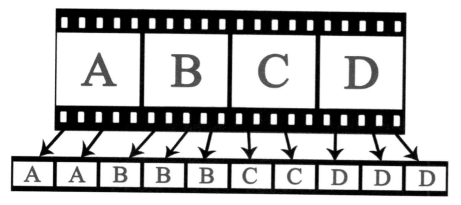

FIGURE 3.9
3:2 pulldown.

which television is broadcast at 59.94Hz, which is the scanning frequency to show 29.97 fps. When converting the video, odd frames will be created through two interlaced frames while even frames will be created by three (see Figure 3.9).

After the telecine process is complete, the 24 progressive frames will result in 60 interlaced fields/second. If this is to be displayed on an interlaced display, no further translation is required. However, if this is to be shown on a 30 progressive frame/second display, then more interpretation is needed. This process is known as reverse-telecine, which interprets that the same frame data stays together when deinterlacing. The algorithm will need to look at multiple frames, essentially doubling some frames. In addition, some non-linear editors will need to apply an inverse telecine which reverts the process back to 24 progressive frames.

REFRESH RATE

As previously mentioned, a film projector advances at a rate of 24 fps. Also, as mentioned, each frame is presented two or three times before advancing. This results in essentially a 48 or 72 Hz refresh rate. With digital video the refresh rate will be in line with 60, 120, or 240 Hz. Simply put, the refresh rate is the speed at which the image is freshly presented to the viewer. Digitally, the refresh rate is the frequency with which a display hardware updates its buffer. When a display is able to refresh the image faster, there is a marked decrease in the appearance of a flicker in the image. Higher frequencies will also help to smooth the transition of film to video.

CHAPTER 4

Display Surface

The display is that which will allow the audience to see the image. When speaking about projection, this will include both the projector and the display surface. There are a variety of methods and display devices ranging from reflective (light reflecting off the surface) and transmissive (light transmitting through the surface) to emissive (light being emitted from the surface) technologies. Even though some of the types of equipment may seem archaic, all are important beyond their historical relevance as they may have continuing use in modern productions.

At first, we will look at the surface itself. The portion of the system that is often neglected, or at least not often considered, is the surface to be projected upon. This could have some impact on emissive displays, but primarily this section will be dedicated to the discussion of the surface for projectors. Generally, a production will use whatever surface is available. Understanding how this affects the image will greatly improve the design. It should be noted that light emanating from the projection surface will always be less than the luminous flux being transmitted from the light engine of a projector. Knowing how much light is lost is critical to the design. As can be seen in Figure 4.1, in a demonstration by Dataton (maker of Watchout

FIGURE 4.1
Reflective and emissive surfaces.

Source: Dataton Watchout

software), images can be effectively combined with different surfaces to create a single display (mixture of LED panels and projection on various geometric surfaces).

SCREEN PROPERTIES

In order to best choose your projection surface, or the best use one that has already been acquired, the designer should understand how to read the design of the material. The importance of each variable will hold different weight depending on the content to be displayed and where the audience will be situated. When you are purchasing a new screen, these variables will be readily available from the manufacturer. Unfortunately, if you have previously acquired material or are using a non-traditional surface, many of these variables will be unknown. With the right measurement equipment, some information can be identified.

Gain

It may seem obvious, but it should be stated that the projection screen is a passive element of the system. It does not *add* light. Instead, a manufactured screen will have controlled optical properties in order to prevent light from becoming fully diffused, which dramatically lessens the amount of light given to the viewer. The measurement of light being transmitted perpendicular from the center of the screen, divided by the luminance of the projector, is known as gain. As has been stated, the human eye is most sensitive to changes in light to dark; having an image that is the correct brightness will be an essential part of the design. If the surface does not transmit that light to the audience, then other parts of the design will need to compensate, potentially to the detriment of the production.

Gain is always used to describe front projection. For rear projection surfaces, gain is known as transmittance, though the calibrated standard is based on the front projection luminance factor equal to one. When a manufacturer is to properly measure a surface, there is a bit more than what a designer will do, but it is good to understand where these measurements come from. The British standard for gain measurement (BS 5382; 1976) states that "a freshly cut surface of magnesium carbonate should be placed centrally and parallel to the surface of the test sample, with the room pitch black and the projector with its luminance at the center of the block measured from a horizontal plane at the center, but at 5 degree horizontal angle from perpendicular. After this measurement is taken, then the block is removed and the screen surface is measured. The resultant measurement is the gain" (L2/L1*100%). As humans perceive a difference in brightness when it is reduced by more than 50%, calculating where the ½ angle of a screen surface is recommended. This is the point from center where the gain is halved.

Contrast Ratio

Display devices will have a contrast ratio associated with them, determined by the amount of light produced versus the amount of light prevented from being shown. A contrast ratio is that comparison between the brightest white and the darkest black of the image. In order to calculate this according to American National Standards Institute (ANSI) standards, a measurement of a checkerboard of 16 alternating black and white rectangles is measured. The ratio is then determined through the average of the white measurements to the average of the black measurements taken from the center of each rectangle. Gain is adversely affected by ambient light as this raises the average of the black levels; thus, a strict control of light spill on the surface is imperative. The lower the eventual contrast, the more difficult it will be for the audience to perceive the image, especially in imagery that is more dependent on that contrast, such as photography. It allows for a separation of tones within the image. A traditional projection screen will be designed with methods of enhancing contrast.

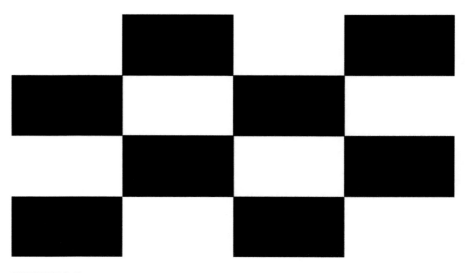

FIGURE 4.2
ANSI contrast checkerboard.

When projecting an image onto a screen, the contrast ratio will be the combination of the projector contrast, the screen contrast, and ambient light on the screen. The greater the contrast ratio in the screen, the less overall light will be returned to the audience, but also it reduces the amount of ambient light interference. It cannot be stressed enough that brightness is the most important part of the human vision system. Improper control of contrast will result in a muted image which will lose the detail necessary for content to be accurately viewed. There is no way to project black; it is simply the absence of light. Any light present, whether from ambient light or poor contrast ratio within the system, will degrade the image.

Contrast is all about information (details of image) and emotion (high contrast can have a different feel and mood than low contrast). It should be noted that there is no target contrast ratio for all content. The system can have a much lower ultimate ratio for general viewership than for watching a motion picture in a cinematic environment. For instance, viewing a presentation in a classroom or at a conference requires a much lower contrast ratio (often targeted at around 15:1) than in the theater, where we often look to see fine detail (50:1 is optimum). These are a far cry from what is often required in cinema with an extreme control over light on the screen, setting the contrast ratio to 80:1. While there will be no standards police coming after the designer of a theatrical performance for not meeting the standards set forth, audiences and critics can be very unforgiving. If the contrast is too low, it is known as flat or soft, which can appear to be less sharp of an image even when in perfect focus. Meanwhile, too high of a contrast is known as hard, which can be jarring and disruptive to some images.

87

Viewing Angle

Knowing where the audience will be viewing the image from is a crucial part of the design. A viewing angle is determined from the center point of the screen in either the horizontal or vertical axis. This is specified in order to guide the optimum brightness from the screen center to either side. In a cinema situation, where the audience is mostly sitting directly in front of the screen, below the level of the projector, the viewing angle does not need to be very great. Conversely, if the audience is situated in a more traditional, radiating pattern, the viewing angle will need to be greater. The consequence of the wrong viewing angle is that the perceived brightness of the image will not be equal to all parts of the audience or that brightness is wasted, potentially contributing to a decrease in contrast due to adding to ambient light.

With a formal projection screen, the viewing angle will be calculated by the manufacturer, giving the designer known variables to work with. This is based on the uniformity of the surface. It will be described as the angle from center in a horizontal plane. As most screens are designed with the audience being in a plane generally no greater than +/–10% vertical, there is no intent for a vertical viewing angle. This could have an impact on a designer in a theater with one or more balconies.

Texture
Screens will be textured to enhance certain characteristics of light. Textures will include lenticular and Fresnel type surfaces, which help to direct the light in particular ways, and at times assist in the rejection of ambient light. The texture will be directionally specific, requiring the screen to be put in a specific orientation to benefit from that texture. Artistically choosing to orient the screen in a different fashion could result in undesirable effects, as noted in the viewing angle designed into particular surfaces.

In addition, textures such as Fresnel were more common on rigid rear projection surfaces than temporary flexible screens.

They are most effective for older rear screen display technologies, which needed greater increase in light transmission. Lenticular and polarized screens are finding favor in designs intended for 3D display. In some office settings, screens are textured to have an increase in ambient light rejection. This is primarily for light coming from above, which is usual in that type of setting. The texture of older, high gain screens can have a negative effect when using high resolution projectors. This can cause a specular aberration, where spots appear throughout the image through the interference of light, as discussed in Chapter 1.

REAR OR FRONT PROJECTION

The majority of projection will be front projection, or having the projector on the same side of the projection surface as the audience. This is often required when the surface is something other than a traditional projection screen. There are benefits and challenges to both methods of displaying the image. Considerations need to include how the surface presents the image to the audience. When looking at a traditional screen, there are a variety of known variables to allow the projection designer to understand how the image should look based on strict calculations. As soon as other theatrical fabrics and set pieces are introduced, the variables become unknown and the designer must build additional flexibility into the system to compensate. As can be seen in Figure 4.3 below, the image is drastically different depending on which material it is on and how much ambient light it is competing with.

Rear Projection

When you are using a rear projection screen, the projector will be situated on the opposite side of the surface with respect to the audience. The light from the projector will transmit through the surface to the audience, resulting in a certain amount of light loss as a portion is reflected back towards the projector.

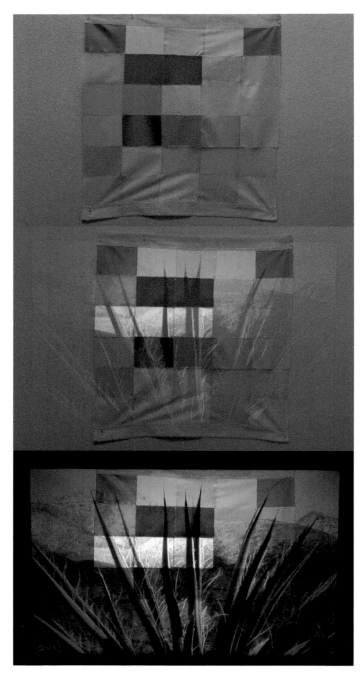

FIGURE 4.3
Examples of different screen materials with a projected image.

The contrast ratio with a rear screen is often better than that of front projection, as it allows light to transmit in both directions. This allows much of the ambient light to pass through the screen, which interferes less with the black levels of the projected image. Another advantage is that the projectionist can at times be a little less precise with the edges of the image, which can be blocked by the frame or soft goods, making setup time faster.

On the other hand, there can be some distinct disadvantages. The biggest issue that plagues this form of display is the amount of unobstructed space required behind the surface. There are a few ways of handling this using front surface mirrors, but small performance areas will always find this challenging (more on this later). Depending on screen material, a rear projected image may suffer from a "hot spot", where the image in the direct path of the projector is bright, and where the remainder of the field diminishes greatly. This can also greatly reduce the viewing angle. Manufactured screens suffer much less from this than alternate materials do. Additionally, positioning of the projector can be more challenging, as short throw lenses have difficulty in being off axis and maintaining an image in focus across the surface.

Front Projection

As previously mentioned, the use of a front projection screen is more common. This method requires the consideration of many factors. Ambient light is the greatest concern for the front projected image. As the front projection surface is designed to reflect light, it cannot differentiate between "good" light and "bad" light. The texture of the surface may help in environments such as the classroom, where the majority of the light is coming from an overhead source. However, ambient light rejecting screens have great difficulty compensating for the multitude of sources in the theater.

A front projection screen can have a much greater range of viewing angles than a rear screen and has the benefit of uniformity in the extent of the image. There are also very specialized screens, including polarized and wavelength rejecting, which aid in enhancing the image and adding to the contrast or even promoting 3D projection. It must be understood that the entirety of the image will be seen by the audience, so great care must be taken by the designer to deal with an image that may not entirely fit the surface, and the accuracy of the projectionist, to accomplish the design.

NON-TRADITIONAL MATERIALS

As opposed to designs for corporate events and other standardized designs, theatrical productions often utilize non-screen materials as the projection surface. This is one of the benefits to using projectors in a media design, as almost anything can be used for the surface. When using non-traditional materials, the designer must be very aware of the physical properties of light in order to realize the design and prepare for the needs of optimizing the image on site. As can be seen in Figure 4.3, the difference in ambient light can change how the image looks.

Some theatrical fabrics will have some known properties in how they handle light. Generally, these properties will often be descriptive of how much light they absorb. These fabrics are not likely to be the projection surface, but may surround the projection area. An example is commando cloth.

The most common material to be projected on will be the muslin drop, often referred to as a cyc (though distinctly different from a traditional cyclorama). It will often be an off-white material, though it has been known to have a light blue hue as well, so color correction may be necessary in the image. Similar to some large screens, the muslin drop can often be made without seams for smaller venues. The material has a regular diffusion across its surface, which has the benefit of a wide viewing angle both vertically and horizontally, but also means that it requires a fairly bright projector in order to have a quality image. As a large surface, it will rarely conform to the aspect ratio of a video projector, so the designer will need to make the decision on whether to attempt to fill the entire surface, which may require some advance techniques, alter the image to allow it to blend into the non-projected areas, or request that carpentry mask it to the size and aspect of the projected image.

Another common fabric will be the theatrical scrim. This material does not have a solid surface, but is a type of mesh. While this offers some challenges when using it, there are some unique advantages. It allows for a front projected image to be displayed, while having the potential for an object to be seen

FIGURE 4.4
Projection on a scrim.

Source: Maureen Selwood

behind it, as seen in Figure 4.4. This effect will require working closely with the lighting designer to pull it off correctly. As this is often used as a lighting effect material, the lighting designer should be able to easily accommodate this request.

Pretty much any material will be able to be used as a front projection surface, as long as the designer understands how well it reflects and diffuses the light and can compensate with bright enough projectors. Some materials will require more trial and error than others, as there will be a discovery of the material properties.

VIDEO AND LED WALLS

In addition to projection surfaces, a variety of emissive displays are a part of media design. These are displays that are not dependent on a surface to display an image, as the surface is what emits the image. There are several different types of displays used for this purpose and there are variations between them.

The monitor is what most people are most familiar with, as it is a part of computer systems used in daily life. In addition to monitors, the next most recognizable emissive display is the LED wall. These are a staple of many music concerts because of their brightness, but can also be seen in a variety of theatrical productions. More detail will be given later about each of these technologies and how to use them.

Not all display sources are equal. Without side by side comparison, the layperson may not be able to detect a difference. In fact, depending on some of the other design factors, it could be difficult for the expert to distinguish between them even when they are side by side. Regardless, as with the projection surface, there are distinct differences that can greatly affect the outcome. Understanding how the image is created can help the designer create an amazing visual experience.

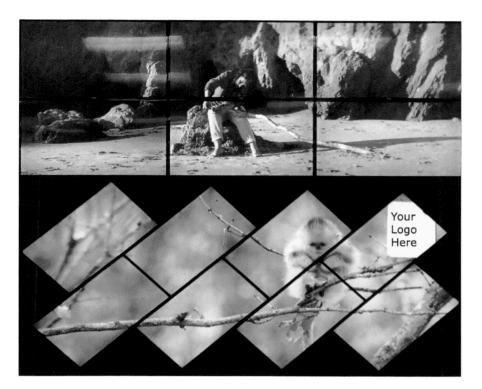

FIGURE 4.5
Example of video wall as digital signage.

Monitor

While the monitor is seen by most of us on a daily basis, there are distinctions among them. A television is a specialized monitor that includes either an analog or a digital tuner to allow for selecting channels. It may or may not be of use to the media designer. In an analog system, this was a variance in the radio frequency (RF) spectrum. This has been altered under the Advanced Television Systems Committee (ATSC), which oversees the transmission of digital television. This will likely be of little importance to the theatrical environment outside of CCTV (closed circuit television is used for monitoring activity in the performance area). What is good to know is that outside of the tuner, the television is just like other monitors that accept some form of video signal and display that on the front surface.

There are differences in how these are created, such as LED, OLED, LCD, plasma (mostly phased out), and the much older CRT. Some will be back lit while others are sidelit. Sidelit monitors will almost never be desired due to the color shift if the surface is not viewed from directly in front. Surfaces will most often be flat, but they could be curved: convex for older CRTs or concave for some newer LEDs. Each will have different benefits and drawbacks which should be considered, but we can only touch the surface (no pun intended), as there are too many variables to discuss in detail here. Common to almost all monitors is glare, which can possibly be avoided when working with the lighting designer.

The CRT was the standard monitor used under NTSC. It was the traditional TV all the way back to the beginning of broadcast television. As these are no longer manufactured, if a designer needs one for a production, he or she will likely be looking at second hand electronics stores or similar situations. Until the past few years, many production studios continued to use them, as they had the best color reference. It is safe to say that this is no longer the case. The CRT should probably not be used unless necessary as they are bulky and heavy, and have a very limited resolution. As all units will be used at this point, it will likely be harder to find units of matching quality.

Another technology that is out of production is the plasma monitor. The surface of these monitors was individual RGB pixels which contained a rare gas that, when excited with electricity, produced light (similar to a fluorescent light). While these had a superior image and rich blacks and wide viewing angles, they had a rough time competing for a few reasons. These monitors were heavy, similar to CRTs, especially in comparison to LED monitors. They were also very fragile in that the slightest crack could allow the gasses to escape, making the monitor useless. Even when they were operational, they often suffered screen burn, where an image that was represented for a long time would leave a ghostly image when changed. To compensate for this, some monitors would shift the pixels of the image on a regular basis, which could be a distraction.

Liquid Crystal Display (LCD) monitors are the most common in use today. These either are sidelit, using a fluorescent light source, or are LED backlit, having the light pass through a liquid crystal medium with RGB filters. The LCDs are very thin and are voltage regulated as to how much light passes through each individual pixel. They can have good color representation, but they can suffer with blacks. Similar to a projected image,

FIGURE 4.6
Video black with a sidelit monitor.

you have to contend with video black as they will always emanate some light. Manufacturers are constantly improving this technology, and there are some reference quality LCD monitors available. These tend to have a limited viewing angle, especially those which are sidelit.

A technology that is also being improved upon and which will likely become more popular is the Organic Light Emitting Diode (OLED). This is a thinner film display which has the potential of replacing other LCDs in the future. This is similar to the plasma monitor in that when electricity is applied, the OLEDs phosphoresce (glow) and provide their own illumination. This means that they can provide truer blacks and offer much better contrast. Since they do not require an extra source of illumination, these are lighter and thinner monitors. As they continue to develop, they are also becoming much more flexible, which could mean that in the future they will be able to be applied to a surface like wallpaper.

Currently, monitors are set in size as individual units. They can be combined when creating a larger display, as seen in Figure 4.5; this is commonly known as a video wall. When creating a video wall, the choice of monitor will generally include the size of bezel, or the "picture frame" surrounding the display area. Monitors which are designed with the purpose of being part of a video wall will have extremely narrow bezels, minimizing the mullion (gap between active display areas), while consumer televisions are likely to have much thicker bezels. In addition, professional models intended to be used as part of a video wall will often have built into their firmware the ability to deconstruct an image to display only a portion, allowing for the total wall to show the complete image. Monitors not designed with this purpose will require additional hardware or software to complete this task. Of course, even if the monitor has the ability to work as part of a video wall on its own, the designer could choose an external hardware or software in order to better meet the needs of the design. Many of these technologies are found in the digital signage market for retail display operations.

Rear Projection

In the era where the CRT reigned supreme, large display monitors were impractical. To increase the size of the display, rear projection televisions were created. These continued in popularity for a while even when much larger flat panel displays were available, as they were generally considerably less expensive. While these have mostly fallen out of favor as other monitor technologies have surpassed the older technology in quality and cost, there are a couple of modern examples which are still being used.

Rear Projection Cube

While rear projection televisions lost favor in the consumer market for their bulk and quality of image, newer versions made their way into the display market. These displays are intended to work together as part of a complete system as opposed to individually, as their predecessors were. Each cabinet will be uniformly designed in order to stack together, similar to other video walls. They all contain their own short throw projector, with all the advantages and disadvantages of such. In addition, their circuitry can allow them to communicate with their neighbors and help match brightness through internal luminance sensors. Generally, they will run on solid state lighting technology to grant them the many hours necessary to run continuously. Also, as they are using projection technology, they can have a very high pixel density, benefitting designs where the audience could be near the display. Also, the mullion is nearly nonexistent, as little as 0.7 mm for some models, giving them a much greater advantage over other video walls.

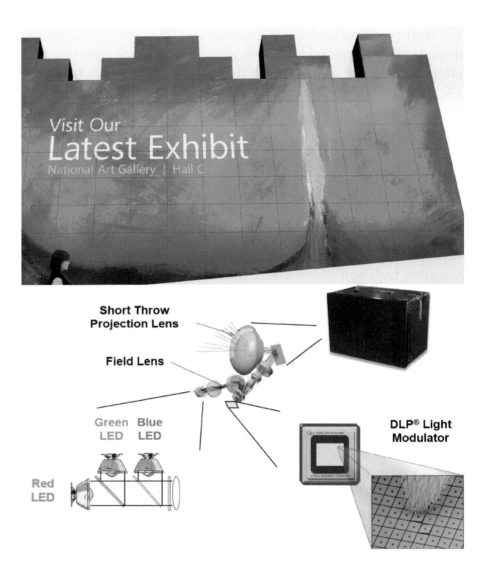

FIGURE 4.7
Christie's MicroTiles is a popular rear projection cube.

Source: Christie Digital Systems

Laser Phosphor Display

Another re-envisioned technology is the laser excitation phosphor display. Older CRT technology used an electron gun to activate phosphors embedded on a screen to create images.

A newer technology, Laser Phosphor Display (LPD) replaces the cathode tube with laser diodes in a similar fashion for displaying images on a phosphor embedded screen. These units are much slimmer and lighter than their CRT ancestors, and also use considerably less power per given area of the display. A significant advantage of the LPD is their size scalability. The

FIGURE 4.8
Prysm LPD tiles.

Source: Prysm, Inc.

modular nature of the laser light engine allows for establishing an end use case determined display of any screen size, by merely racking and stacking an array of light engines. These have mainly been used to create video walls for digital signage or use in control rooms, but could be of unique interest for a designer who may be looking for a long-lasting, large-format solution within an entertainment venue.

Panel

When the designer wishes to create a larger, more seamless display, the choice is generally to use an array of LED panels, creating what is known as a LED wall. These panels are either solid or open spaced and will have the individual LEDs spaced at regular intervals. The benefit is that they can be configured in many different orientations to give the designer exactly the size of display desired. This is generally a very expensive option when looking to create a large image, as compared to projection, but has the ability to compete with high amounts of ambient light. This will often even allow for daytime use.

The spacing between the LEDs is known as pixel pitch. The lower the number, the more tightly they are spaced, granting higher resolution. Tighter pixel pitch will be required the closer the audience is to the display. The greater distance that the viewer is from the display, the more space can be allowed between pixels, and the perception will be the same. In addition, the type of image that is being created may determine the pixel pitch. The more detail required, such as photographic representation, the tighter the pitch required. Each pixel of a panel is made up of multiple LED sources covered with a lens. As seen in Figure 4.9, sometimes individual colors are doubled in order to better represent color as a whole.

Video walls differ from LED walls in that the LED panels are only designed to work together to create a display. While the

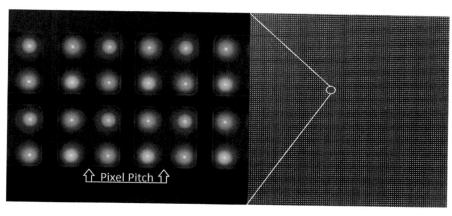

FIGURE 4.9
Pixel pitch.

panels will have a set number of pixels, these do not correspond to specific computer resolutions. When combined together, they can make common resolutions or can greatly depart from them to fill the image space as envisioned in the design. The display in Figure 4.10 shows a 1920x1080 output with a white display (note that some were still being color matched) and the top portion with the color bars is just as wide, but is not 1080 high. This required multiple media servers to create one image.

Outside of the performance space, LED panels are often seen as digital billboards. This is where a designer can see the challenges of using them. In a long-running production or with rentals from companies who use them in many different situations, additional challenges can arise. In a projected display or video wall, when a portion of the image fails to display, it is usually single pixels. With the LED wall, entire sections of the panels will fail, leaving a cluster of pixels missing from the image (note the black area in the white image). These can be replaced. However, the replacement will have some differences from the rest of the wall (note the variance in white). In some cases, especially when used outdoors, the physical panel will be a different color, which is noticeable in areas of contrast (see the front section of the

FIGURE 4.10
Example of LED wall.

wall in Figure 4.11). In addition, the color of the diodes can be different, which require calibration to match colors to those of nearby panels. Depending on the manufacturer of the panels, there will be various levels of ability to color match and it may require considerable time to do so.

FIGURE 4.11
The back and front of an LED wall.

As LED panels do not require any additional screen for the display to be seen, the viewer is looking directly at the light source. This allows additional flexibility in how the panels are designed. Often for indoor displays, and outdoor displays with a sturdy structure, the surface will be solid and not allow the audience to view what is behind the panels (as in the wall above). However, when designing for an outdoor production where a solid structure may have difficulty contending with air movement, many panels will have openings, which allow airflow. Obviously, this will cause some issue with what is seen behind, potentially requiring an additional light blocking surface behind the panels. On the other hand, some panels will have virtually no structure between pixels, creating an almost transparent image. Figure 4.12 is an excellent example of this type of panel, where you can clearly see the image but also see behind the panels. With the proper lighting, this could emulate the use of theatrical scrim.

FIGURE 4.12
LED wall with open space between pixels.

Another benefit that the LED wall will have over other video walls is that some panels will have flexibility in their surface. While a video wall can have separation in individual displays, creating a more dynamic and interesting video surface to view, they cannot truly fit a curve. With some LED panels, the surface will actually allow the panels to curve to create a more visually striking surface.

Transparent Display

A number of manufacturers have created displays which look like a window pane, in that they are visually transparent but

FIGURE 4.13
Transparent display used in retail situation.

also act as a video monitor. Although these were developed with retail situations in mind, they could have expanded use for special effect video in live performance. The designer will need to look at the benefit as compared to cost, as this could add considerably to the budget. However, effects similar to Pepper's Ghost may be created without requiring a projector and screen, plus it will require considerably less space to accomplish the effect. On the other hand, display panel sizes are limited (note the division in panels in Figure 4.13).

Electrowetting and Electrophoretic Technology
Once known only for handheld display devices for reading digital copies of books and magazines, these technologies are getting bigger and may find their way into the live performance

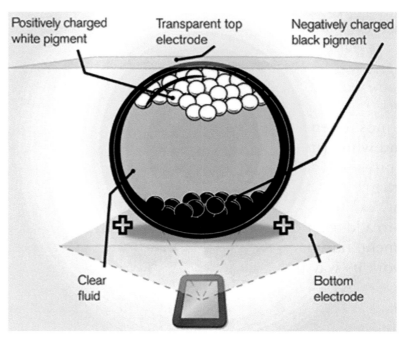

FIGURE 4.14
How electrophoretic technology works.

Source: E Ink Corporation

market once the price and availability are right. While these are mainly passive reflective devices, not actively producing light, they may be able to be sidelit or backlit. As they are not natively producing light, this technology would require working with the lighting department to make the image seen. They have a good viewing angle, similar to paper. These technologies could truly replace painted backdrops.

Electrophoretic technology is commonly known as E ink or electronic ink. It has its roots back in the 1970s when researchers from manufacturers such as Xerox were looking at an electronic alternative to ink on paper. Individual cells have particles that are positively or negatively charged, which are moved around by a charge beneath them. This can even provide split cells if different charges are placed on different halves of each cell. The technology is also known as bistable, meaning that the image on the surface remains when power is removed; the only use of power is during the change of the image. For this reason, electronic book readers that use E ink displays will have a much better battery life than the ones that use LED or LCD displays.

109

E ink is most often seen as a two pigment system, creating a black and white (not monochrome) image. This technology cannot provide video, but still images could be mixed with appropriate lighting to create a landscape. It can be applied to very thin flexible display film which may provide other opportunities to add texture. This is limited to paper-size surfaces at the moment, but that would not preclude its use, as it could likely work its way into props for magical effects. There are offerings for color E ink, but at this time this is only suited for static images, as it has a very slow refresh rate and the entire surface must change at once.

A similar type of reflective display is through the use of colored oils in a process called electrowetting. As opposed to using

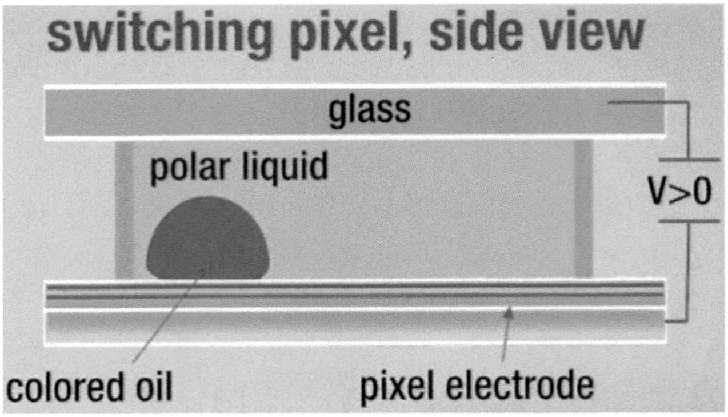

FIGURE 4.15
How electrowetting technology works.

Source: Etulipa

positive and negative charges, it uses varying voltage between a liquid and an electrode beneath a hydrophobic insulator. As this is a reflective surface, this technology uses subtractive color mixing using CMY (cyan, magenta, and yellow), starting with a white surface and working towards black as the colors are applied. This is the process of color printing. Each cell will contain the three different layers of colored oils. It uses the physical principal of surface tension of each of the liquids. By applying various voltages to the layers, the oils contract or spread out across the cell, allowing for color mixing. Similar in design to LED panels, at least one European manufacturer is making this technology with the ability to combine multiple panels into large displays that can be used as billboards, even covering the sides of buildings, at about 1/100th the power consumption. It provides rich colors and has refresh speeds fast enough for use for video. As this is a new technology, it may be cost prohibitive to develop into theatrical use at this time, but will certainly find its place in the near future.

CHAPTER 5

Projectors

Projected images are ephemeral. They live in another dimension, and dance in a way that is like music and poetry.

~Wendall Harrington

The most common new media display technology used for live performance is the video projector. It is the tool of choice for its flexibility and cost, especially when creating very large images. While it can have a high cost, it is often the least expensive option for large displays. If the designer is working in a house that owns its equipment, then he or she will work with whatever is available. Upon initially looking at a projector it would be difficult to tell one apart from another. However, there are slight differences for the designer between the technologies used in the projector. Understanding these slight differences may make the difference, depending on certain other design choices.

The video projector has made tremendous advancements over its predecessor, the film projector. With the explosion of computing industry, the drive to display digital images has developed along with it. Early digital projectors were not generally accepted in entertainment due to lack of brightness, the expense, and the skill necessary to operate them. In the latter half of the 1990s, this rapidly began to change due to advancements in both the convention and cinema industries. Brightness and resolution, along with greater ease of use—such as internally converged images—made them more attractive to the entertainment industry. With the turn of the century came prices that continued to bring digital video projectors into the budgets of smaller productions. Computing power has continued to grow, allowing for more complex images to be created live, escaping from the hold of the pre-recorded image. The projector's popularity has inspired a push which has increased creativity, pushing the bounds of what is possible.

There are many different technologies that come into play when considering a projector. The two main components to consider for presentation are the type of light source and the type of image creation technology. Other considerations for the designer will include lens type, input type, resolution, contrast ratio, and color accuracy. What technology is chosen will depend on what is most important to the design.

HISTORICAL DEVICES

It is important to note some of the technology prior to video projection because it is what encouraged the development of the modern digital projector. Some of the early design properties that made it popular are the same reasons that it is popular today. So, the modern designer may find it useful to study historical uses from the Victorian era onward for inspiration. It should be reiterated that video projectors are not the only tool for the media designer, and some historical devices may serve well in the types of image created and budget of the production, as well as the possibility of being fit for the job.

Cathode Ray Tube

This is very unlikely to be used in the modern realm of projection technology and so will only be briefly mentioned. The CRT projector design was more prevalent in rear projection

TV, but was also used in older "three gun" projectors, where the convergence of the three primary colors is accomplished with three separate lenses. Each time the projector was set up, the red, green, and blue parts of the display would need to be converged. This required a flat projection surface and a considerable amount of time setting up. They were very dim and could not achieve higher brightness. They also used a considerably high amount of energy to obtain images of only a few hundred lumens. These projectors were greatly dependent on the screen material used. Much of the developments in screen gain technology were to make use of almost every bit of light produced by these projectors. Many of those developments are no longer necessary and can even come as a detriment to high resolution, high brightness modern projectors. Advances in technology have rendered these completely obsolete and they would only be used if required by a script.

PROJECTOR ANATOMY

A projector, just like any other machine, is a set of components which work together. There are some commonalities and some distinct differences between models of projector. These differences may be so subtle to the casual user that this section can be skipped entirely. However, for the designer who has an eye for specific detail, these differences can take a design from good to great.

The brains of a projector may be fully integrated on a single motherboard, as is the case with many home theater and business class projectors. On the other hand, in the rental/staging business, projectors are often designed modularly in order to accommodate a wider variety of options as well as ease of field repair. For these, there are a variety of control boards, some of which are hot swappable to allow for repair while the projector is running. These will separate out the control over fans and power with the central firmware, image processing, and other individual control. Some projectors will be considerably more powerful in the ways in which they can process the signal. There are potentials for reshaping the image and combining multiple images, as well as displaying 3D images. How each manufacturer breaks up this control can be drastically different.

What makes more of a difference to the designer is the way the image is ultimately produced. The final image is dependent on two main factors, the optic train and the light source. There are a variety of light sources which all create light in different ways. Because the quality of the light is different, this will affect the final outcome. Beyond the light source is a set of lenses, reflectors, filters, and prisms which shape the light and create the final projected image. There are benefits and drawbacks to each of these and it cannot be said that there is one that is ultimately better than another, just one that might be better for a specific use than another.

LCD

The Liquid Crystal Display (LCD) has been the workhorse of the digital projection world due to its relatively low cost and wide availability. The image is created by light being split into three primary colors (in rare cases, it is split into yellow as well) through a series of dichroic mirrors, which allow some wavelengths of light to pass through while others are reflected. The colored light is then passed through polarizing filters and LCD panels before the colors are combined within in a compound prism, to be focused by the lens. The panel will either absorb the light or allow it to pass through at each pixel. Of the digital technologies, it most closely represents historical projectors by allowing light to pass through the medium.

That is the simplified version. LCD technology actually encompasses a variety of technologies, for there is not a single type of

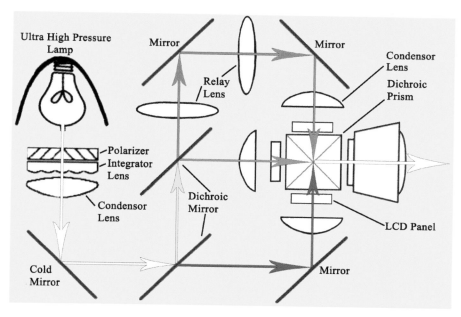

FIGURE 5.1
LCD optic path.

LCD display. There are passive technologies used in watches, calculators, and some telephone screens, but projectors use active technologies. In some monitor displays and simple micro projectors, a simple Thin-Film Transistor (TFT) LCD is used. More commonly for high brightness LCD projectors, there is a variant TFT known as High Temperature Poly-Silicon (HTPS) panels. These have a higher pixel density and contrast ratio than other LCD products.

Typically, LCD projectors use a High Intensity Discharge (HID) lamp for the light source. The light from the lamp is immediately condensed through specialized lenses. Some manufacturers will immediately begin the polarization of the light at this point, which ultimately improves performance. Through the integrator lenses, the light is shaped to the size of the panel. This process evens out the light and reduces light loss. Then, the light goes through a series of dichroic mirrors,

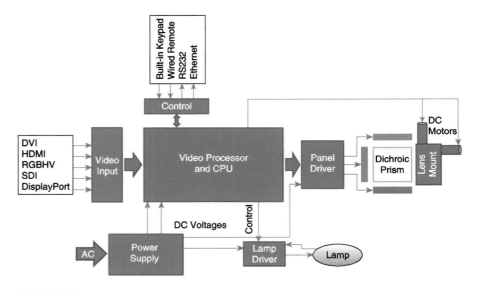

FIGURE 5.2
Block diagram of a typical LCD projector.

which reflect certain wavelengths, but allow others to pass through. Those that pass will encounter secondary dichroic mirrors to complete the process.

Each of the three (select models add yellow as a fourth) separated colors will be focused on their respective LCD panel. Just prior to the panel will be a polarized filter. This adjusts the light to a specific wave direction. Think of a polarized filter as louvers: the light that is going in the right direction gets through easily, while the filter minimizes or absolutely rejects the light in different wave patterns. Thus, the LCD panel in its "off" state will block nearly all light, as it will be 90 degrees rotated from the filter. To allow light to pass, during the "on" state, the appropriate pixels on the LCD panel will align themselves with the polarized light. In order to achieve various levels of grey within the light, this will cycle many times per second.

After the light has passed through the LCD, it will recombine in a dichroic prism. This cube shaped prism has internal dichroic surfaces to reflect the colored light to the lens. Each LCD panel is aligned so that the image which passes through to the prism will be precisely converged as it goes through the lens.

FIGURE 5.3
LCD panels and dichroic prism.

Source: David Susilo

At this time, brightness is limited to 15,000 lumens in a single projector using multiple HID lamps and likely will not exceed this. With solid state light sources such as laser illumination, there may be the possibility to surpass this. However, with the prevalence of HID lamp technology being used, this is what the designer should consider first. Over a period of time, the polarized filters and LCD panels will tend to degrade, allowing colored light to pass through when not desired. This is due to the absorption of the unwanted light and is known as "burn through". Projector maintenance can have an influence on how soon that happens. Proper maintenance will be discussed more in Chapter 10.

Another item for a designer to consider with this technology is that it offers a substantial delineation between pixels, creating what can be described as a "screen door" effect. This is especially noticeable when the image is large and the audience is close to the surface. With higher resolutions and smaller display areas, this is less evident.

FIGURE 5.4
Visible separation between pixels will diminish with the correct sizing and distance to viewer.

DLP

The second most common method of displaying an image is the DLP. Digital Light Processing, or DLP, a technology developed by Texas Instruments, has two different means of displaying the image, but both incorporate the use of the Digital Micromirror Device (DMD). The two methods are either the single-chip DLP or the three-chip DLP. There is the added benefit that, at least with three-chip models, brightness seems to be limited only by the illumination method. Currently, some cinema projectors with solid state illumination have exceeded 60,000 lumens.

FIGURE 5.5
Image of DMD.

119

The DMD is a micro-display device which uses an array of extremely tiny mirrors (notice what looks like glitter in the above picture; those are individual mirrors), which are situated on a CMOS memory chip. These mirrors, which are the individual pixels of the image, are individually controlled in a bistable spatial manner to reflect the light in one of two directions. The grey scale is created by the rapid switching of the position of the mirrors, typically plus or minus 10 to 12 degrees. Typically, DLP projectors are able to obtain greater black levels than their LCD counterparts. This is due to the light path not being initially directed towards the lens; thus errant light remains within the unit. Also, the compact nature of the mirrors greatly minimizes the screen door effect seen in LCD projectors.

Single-Chip

For many home theater and business class projectors, customers looking to get a DLP projector will likely be looking at a single-chip model. The primary advantage is that its color purity will last much longer over the life of the projector than that of an LCD, and a DLP generally falls within the same price range as an LCD for comparable brightness. The single-chip image utilizes only a single DMD. In order to have a color image, white light is passed through a synchronized color wheel and then is either reflected through the lens or to a light trap in the projector. There are a variety of different color wheels that a manufacturer may use depending on the colors which may be most represented. Each color wheel will be segmented differently, not relying solely on primary colors.

As we saw back in Figure 1.14 of a standard chromaticity diagram, we saw the range of typical human vision. The area marked

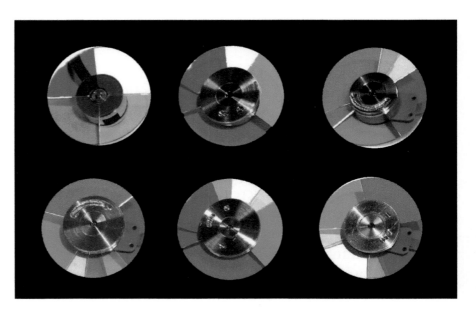

FIGURE 5.6
A sample of color wheels.

within it is the color range that a typical display is capable of. This range can be changed by the manufacturer by changing a color wheel, a sampling of which can be seen in Figure 5.6. When color rendering is critical, the designer should find the projector that easily matches the spectrum needed.

Just after the color wheel, the light is shaped by an integrator rod. From here, there are two methods of getting the light to the DMD and out to the lens. The first optic path uses a Total Internal Reflectance (TIR) prism. This is similar to what will be used on the three-chip models yet to be discussed. This is known as a telecentric optical system. The nontelecentric optical system instead uses a series of mirrors and lenses to direct the light to the DMD. Telecentric designs tend to allow for a more compact design and can have more even field, though not as dark of black levels. Nontelecentric designs are less expensive (due to the cost of precision needed for the TIR prism) and have better keystone correction (less aberration). There are a number of additional advantages and disadvantages that manufacturers can utilize when choosing between these two designs, but they are less important to the end user.

121

The greatest advantage that the single-chip projector has over others is that the convergence is always perfect, since all of the pixels are created by a single chip. On the other hand, a unique effect which can be observed by small minority of viewers is called a "rainbow effect". This happens when the motion in the frame rate exceeds the ability for the projector to fully realize the entire color of each frame. Thus, fast-moving objects may have incorrectly colored artifacts.

Generally, a designer will choose brightness and contrast over color as he or she will know that color will ultimately need to be adjusted on site, as there are additional variables which will come into play. We will discuss this in Chapter 9. Since

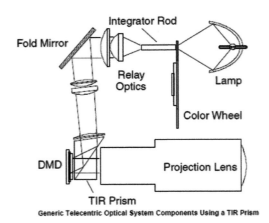

Generic Telecentric Optical System Components Using a TIR Prism

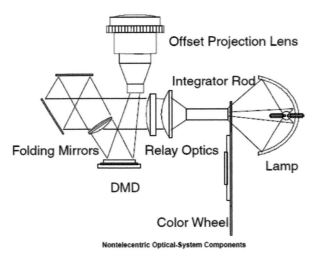

Nontelecentric Optical-System Components

FIGURE 5.7
Telecentric and nontelecentric optical paths.

brightness is measured with a full white field, the end user may feel that a single-chip DLP does not appear to be as bright when displaying an image as the comparably bright LCD projector. Color brightness will have a steep decline in this technology. Consider that with a four segment wheel (the most basic color wheel), a single primary color could only be displayed 25% of the time as compared to a three-chip (or three-panel LCD) will show that same color 100% of the time. Since the brightness is regulated by the amount of time light is allowed to pass to the screen, then that brightness is greatly diminished by not being present. This is most evident in a side by side comparison.

Three-Chip

As projection is often competing with stage lighting, brighter projectors are generally needed to cover the area required for a production. Instead of using a color wheel, this type of projector splits the light into the three primaries through the use of a compound TIR prism. Unlike the LCD, which uses a series of dichroic mirrors, the three-chip DLP uses the TIR prism to split, direct, and recombine the light to create the image. This allows for a uniformly bright image regardless of color. Similar to the single-chip DLP, light is either reflected through the lens or inside to a light trap, which absorbs the energy. This grants the DLP a greater ability to have a greater contrast ratio.

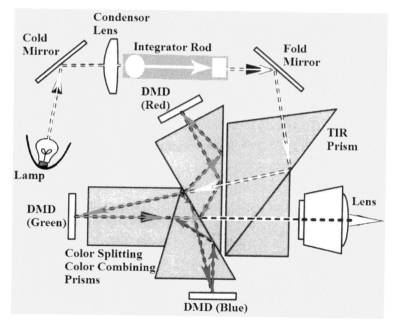

FIGURE 5.8
Three-chip DLP optical path.

These projectors use a number of different illumination technologies to achieve the higher brightness. The optic path may vary, but usually has similar design. The DMD can be sensitive to heat, which can cause premature failure. In order to prevent this, infrared radiation (IR) is filtered out as soon as possible. Light from the lamp will be filtered by what is known as a cold mirror. This is a dichroic mirror which allows the IR to pass through, to be dissipated by a heat sink. The remainder of the light passes through the integrator rod, which shapes it to the size and dimensions of the DMDs. The light is then reflected off a fold mirror, a dichroic mirror which filters out much of the ultraviolet light, to the TIR prism. The prism will have the three DMDs connected directly to it. Two of these will be adjustable by a qualified technician to properly converge the three colors.

This technology is the preferred choice of manufacturers for building the brightest model projectors for the rental/staging market as well as the cinema market. It is the choice of many designers for color purity and length of service. Producers may not think it is as great, since this tends to be the most expensive projection technology.

LCOS

Liquid Crystal on Silicon (LCOS) is somewhat of a hybrid, using LCD panels to still absorb the unwanted light, but then with a silicon reflective surface behind, which reflects the image, similar to a DLP system. Some manufacturers have specific technologies that they use to improve on the basic technology, and thus call their variations by different names. For instance, JVC calls theirs D-ILA (Direct-Drive Image Light Amplification), while Sony calls theirs SXRD (Silicon X-tal Reflective Display). This technology tends to not have any lower resolution models and can be the most expensive.

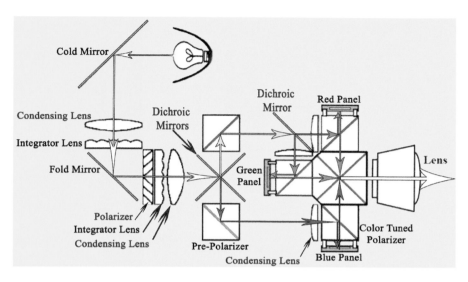

FIGURE 5.9
LCOS optic path.

As can be seen in Figure 5.9, the optic path has few similarities to the LCD. Light is condensed similarly. However, how beams are split and recombined varies quite a bit from LCDs. While single panel models were experimented on, few of them came to the projector market. In addition, the speed of the panels is less than that of the single-chip DLP.

LCOS projectors have tended to perform better in terms of contrast ratios than LCD or DLP projectors. The contrast difference is in the white to black ratio in the same image, but also in the full screen video black. In addition, the space between pixels tends to be the smallest, giving it the most even image. This means that it all but completely avoids the screen door effect. Also, this technology can support much brighter light sources than LCD, as there are currently 4K cinema projectors with at least 30,000 lumens.

ILLUMINATION TECHNOLOGY

After understanding how the light is turned into an image, it is good to understand the light source. The quality of the light is most important when color rendering is critical. This is not limited to making sure the designer gets a particular hue, but also applies when using multiple projectors to create a larger image (blending) or where the same image is shown on multiple surfaces. Most projectors will use some form of lamp, though lamp-free technologies utilizing solid state illumination are becoming more widely available.

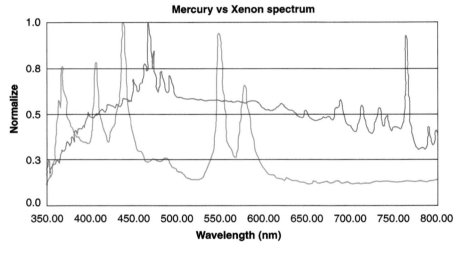

FIGURE 5.10

HID vs. Xenon color intensity.

Source: Christie Digital

Metal Halide

The HID lamp is used in the majority of projectors. These are also known as Metal Halide or Mercury-Vapor lamps, and Philips manufactures the Ultra High Performance (UHP) lamp, but they are all similar in construction. They can be used individually or in tandem (up to four in a single projector) for greater brightness. These lamps can be pressurized up to several hundred atmospheres, which allows them to be fairly compact. They do contain mercury, as the one name suggests, which requires limited disposal based on local jurisdictions. In addition, there is the rare occurrence that they may explode during use. If so, precaution needs to be taken during the cleanup process.

Manufacturers use a metric known as the Color Rendering Index (CRI) to measure the color rendition of a light source. As can be seen in Figure 5.10, HID lamps typically have very spiky color ranges. This can limit the colors that the projector can produce, depending on how it is calibrated. With LCD and three-chip DLP projectors, much of the light spectrum is filtered in the optic path and the dichroics will be designed to utilize the maximum wavelengths and to balance the CRI with the originally specified lamp. However, this often reduces the overall light output. In addition, as the lamp ages, these spikes are less pronounced, which will result in an apparent color shift in the output of the projector. When projectors are used individually, this may be subtle enough not to be noticed, but when multiple projectors are used to create one larger image or multiple projection surfaces are in close relation, the color difference can be quite noticeable, to the point of distraction.

These lamps have relatively good energy efficiency as compared to brightness. This depends a lot on how much light is wasted in getting the proper color rendition. They also have been able to obtain long lamp life. Under normal use, many manufacturers have stated 2,000 hours of standard operation and even greater life when in "eco mode", where the lamps are not driven as hard. The greater efficiency of the lamp means that they also run cooler, reducing the amount of fan noise associated with cooling the projector.

Xenon

In higher brightness projectors, the choice is often the Xenon lamp. Similar to the metal halide lamp, it utilizes an arc of electric current between an anode and a cathode to create heat and illuminate the gasses contained in the envelope. However, as seen above, the color rendition is considerably better, as the overall spectrum is better represented. Also, the color image is better retained as the lamp ages.

Xenon lamps are generally larger than their counterparts. In addition, there is a greater gap between the anode and cathode, requiring a greater amount of energy to create and maintain the arc. Unlike cinema projectors, which require the bare lamp to be installed in the projector (similar to a Xenon follow spot), most projectors will use a lamp module. This makes installation simple, similar to the mercury-vapor lamps. They generally have a lower lamp life, averaging around 750 hours, and have a greater cost per lamp. To offset this cost, some manufacturers allow the end user, with the proper training, to reuse the lamp housing by installing a new bare "bubble lamp" bulb. While this is more environmentally safe, there still exists a danger, since the lamp is under extreme pressure and there is the possibility of an explosion, especially while the lamp is in use.

As these lamps age, they have a considerable drop in brightness. Near the end of its life expectancy, the Xenon lamp will likely only be emitting half of its initial output. In addition, they are more susceptible to changes in power. Too low of power to the projector can cause a weakening of the arc, resulting in a noticeable flicker in the image. Too high of power can overheat the gasses, causing the envelope to blue, causing light loss. Finally, a weak seal will, at some point during use, cause a fairly rapid failure, blackening the envelope. Due to their higher power needs, these projectors may cause difficulty if the performance space is not able to provide the necessary power.

Solid State—LED, Laser Phosphor, 3P Laser

As projectors are becoming more widely used in increasing applications, the need for greater efficiency and ease of use is equally increasing. Projectors are being used in more situations where trained technicians are less available to attend to them, and they are being used more often, including continuous use in commercial displays. An increasingly popular solution is to replace the lamp with solid state illumination. They start up very fast and can be moved immediately after shutting down (lamps require a cool down period). Some run cool enough to work without any fans at all, making them extremely quiet and easy to maintain.

Light Amplification by Stimulated Emission of Radiation (laser) is a term we all understand as extremely concentrated light. The general public generally knows of lasers as aids in identification (for example, the laser pointer) or some high tech weapon. However, the laser and the LED are the two main sources of providing illumination as an alternative to the two main lamp technologies. When using these technologies to create light, projector manufacturers have to make some significant adaptations prior to the LCD or DMD in the projector. These technologies can be used in tandem or individually, in a variety of combinations.

The LED, strictly on its own, is not a very bright projector. As a source of illumination, LEDs are popular in the pico projector market (small, very portable projectors) as the low power consumption can allow them to even run on battery power. Some are small enough to be included as part of other systems, such as cameras or phones. They can also compare to some home theater projectors, at around 1,000–2,000 lumens. They often are paired with LCD or LCOS imaging systems but are not excluded from DLP. They have very specific colors which they emit, making them very efficient in how the projector uses the light. They have an extremely long life at anywhere between 10,000 and 100,000 hours of use (typically on the lower end). Often the LED source is not replaceable, as it should last the life of the projector. As opposed to lamps, they have little change in their color over their life and maintain their brightness for much longer.

On the other side of things, there is the laser projector. This is not the style of projector used in planetariums or concerts, where the scanning laser rapidly creates patterns. Instead, in a three color laser system, they simply replace the light from a typical lamp source. Similar to the LED, the laser has a very narrow range of the light spectrum. Due to this, both of them can have a greater color range displayed than lamp based systems, as well as very strong contrast ratios. Laser based projectors can be extremely bright through the tandem use of multiple sources. For ultra-bright projectors (over 35,000 lumens), the light source is typically located outside the projector, with the combined light being fed to the projector via fiber optic umbilical. Unlike the LED system, the pure laser projector does require a considerable amount of cooling, which can be an additional advantage of having the separated illumination system.

Not all laser projectors use multiple lasers to create white light. In the mid-brightness projectors, from around 3,500 to a maximum of about 12,000 lumens, the laser phosphor system is used. In this system, a blue laser provides the source of illumination. Similar to a single-chip DLP, the color of the light needs to be changed to produce a full range of colors. This is accomplished in one of three ways.

The typical laser phosphor shines a blue laser on a phosphor wheel, which in turn creates yellow light, while a space will allow the blue to shine through (similar to white light shining through a color wheel). Then using a color wheel, red and green are subtracted from the yellow, which allows for four primary colors to be mixed for the final image. The next version is similar to the typical version, but adds a red LED in order to boost the red light source. The final version uses a red laser instead of a red LED to produce even more saturated colors.

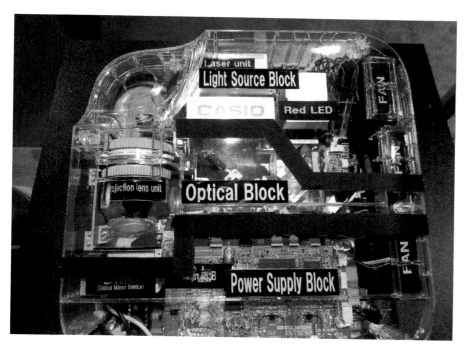

FIGURE 5.11
A Casio laser phosphor projector.

LENSES

The final component of the projector anatomy is the lens. This is just as critical a component as all other portions of the optic system. This is what is going to determine the size of the image and how far away the projector can be, as well as how much light will be lost. Projector lenses are essentially designed with two specifications, the focal length and F-stop. The latter is more in the design and less in what will be specified when choosing a lens (throw distance is most often what is desired). The F-stop designates how much light passes through the lens and is determined by the aperture versus the focal length ratio of the lens. The focal length is the ratio between the image size and throw distance. The size of the image-producing element divided by the image size is equal to the throw distance divided by the focal length.

When you are choosing a lens, or reading the information about the non-changeable lens installed in a projector, the first notation that is available is generally the throw ratio. There may be two ratios available on the lens, which correlate to the lens being used with different aspect ratios. It will also notate if the lens is a fixed or zoom lens (possibly notating short or long throw zoom). This ratio is a tool for the designer to determine the size of the image as compared to the distance between the lens and the surface. The size being determined is the width of the image. For the most accurate measurements, use the lens calculator provided by the manufacturer. Professional model projectors will usually have the lenses manufactured by quality lens manufacturers with a history of precision (Canon, Minolta, and many others). This will provide a greater clarity of image than lenses in many of the consumer model projectors. Due to this, the lenses themselves can add thousands of dollars to the purchase price of the projector, but will also retain their value long after the projector has aged into obscurity. There are a few more considerations, which will be discussed in Chapter 9.

Fixed Lens

If the designer is familiar with commodity consumer projectors, many of them will have a lens which cannot be changed and will have a fixed throw distance. What this means is that the throw ratio will force the user to move the projector closer to the surface for a smaller image and farther away for a larger image. The projector will then have a means of focusing the image within the parameters of overall image size range. The projector can make as large an image as possible by continually moving it away from the surface, but there will be a point at which it can no longer accurately focus the image. Cheaper consumer projectors may not give the throw ratio at all, just the maximum projected image size.

Professional model projectors often give the end user the ability to change lenses as to what suits their needs. The projection designer may choose a fixed lens even when not using a consumer model projector. Often the fixed lens will be a short throw, or a lens that allows the projector to be close to a 1:1 ratio. This may be the only available means to achieve a rear projected image due to space constraints. Even though there are short throw zoom lenses, the optical quality of the fixed lens will often be superior. There are some fixed long throw lenses available as well (greater than 5:1 ratio). The benefit is usually in the F-stop value.

133

Zoom Lens

In large venue projectors, the standard lens will most always be a zoom lens. In this instance, the notation of the throw ratio will have a variable on the front end, such as 1.5–2.0:1. This means that the image size will be roughly one and a half times to twice the distance between the lens and the screen as the image is wide. The further away the projector needs to be from the surface, the higher the initial number will need to be to maintain the same size image. As HD images are wider than SD images, the same lens will have a smaller throw ratio for the HD image.

CHAPTER 6

Source

What would a media system be without content? Not much. We would likely be displaying a blank screen or possibly the logo of the display manufacturer, maybe even a classic "Please Stand By". In any case, none of these scenarios are desirable. Previously we discussed the content and the display, but now we will explain the method of playback.

ANALOG SOURCE

With certain analog medium, the source of the display is quite obvious, such as in film or slides. There are variations within these forms that are evident when observing them closely. These variations include anamorphic images or different stock size. When we move to digital sources, it can be much more mysterious to the casual user. Depending on the full system design, it is possible to mix analog and digital sources to some degree as long as they are all electronic signals. However, the designer will most often stick with one type of source for ease of use. A media server is the source of choice most often, but there are many options available. The entirety of the system may have many components or very simply a cable between the source and display. A lot of factors will go into this portion of the design. Then the elements remaining are the distribution system, the means of control, and a possible network of communication.

As was previously mentioned, some of these become components of the display, such as slides or film. There may be reasons why the designer has chosen an analog source such as these, but for the purpose of discussing modern approaches, those technologies will not be covered in detail. Generally speaking, an analog medium is tied to a single display; in other words it cannot be shared simultaneously. Some analog sources, such as magnetic tape stock, can be distributed electronically among multiple displays. This allows flexibility in design. However, an appropriate distribution system needs to be designed due to the degradation of the signal and potential for interference. In addition, different signals can be carried over the same cables and connections, with co-axial cable being the most common. It is imperative to understand that the signal is not changed if the physical cable termination is simply adapted. We will go into this in detail later on.

The most often used medium for analog signal distribution was magnetic tape. While consumers chose the VHS standard over Beta, that wasn't necessarily so in the professional world. The angle at which the tape runs over the player head determines how much information can be stored. The shallower angle of the Beta system allowed much more information to be stored on the tape, thus requiring much more tape for the same length of video. This was one of the reasons that consumers chose VHS, as the Beta system could require two tapes for a feature length movie. Tape stock was a preferred method, as the operator could accurately cue a specific point in the video for playback.

While magnetic tape is rarely used today outside of corporate presentations, it should be noted that it was also adapted to digital systems. Some digital codecs were created with magnetic tape stock in mind. DVcam was not only used for professional cameras, but was also converted into a miniature tape format for consumer camcorders. While this will very likely not enter the entertainment market if it is not already in place, it is good to be aware of this as there are some broadcast technologies which could still use it.

FIGURE 6.1
Professional tape and disc systems.

DIGITAL SOURCE

Digital images have no physical representation other than the storage medium. They are very dependent on all parts of the system being able to communicate with one another. The biggest benefit to the designer is that digital sources have greater flexibility for change, even being able to do so live. A digital source can be established for random access, breaking away from the need for linearity, which will be essential for more complex interactive designs. Also, the digital video projectors are designed with a digital signal in mind, which produces a better image if the projector is receiving data from a digital source than an analog source.

TAPE BASED AND OPTICAL DISK SYSTEMS

When capturing content, the designer may choose to use a camera based system. Camcorders—both professional and consumer versions—used tape based recording for many years.

Some cameras do record directly to an optical disk while most now record to a solid state media. Generally, the recorded media will not be used directly during the actual performance. Instead, the captured images will be edited and transferred to another medium. However, the broadcast industry does have a number of tape players which would still be suited for cueing and playback of the content for a performance if needed.

In addition, optical disk systems, such as DVD and Blu-ray, will likely not be used outside of a film festival or similar performance. However, as there are so many different possibilities for system design, they still need mentioning. Optical disks have the benefit of rapid selection if each cue is set as a chapter on the disk. However, as the method of compression does not always favor the media being paused, instant playback may not be possible. In addition, few players were designed to not show on-screen control options (such as pause, play, etc.). Thus an additional switcher will likely be required to prevent control options from being displayed to the audience.

137

Blu-ray, the high definition optical disk playback method, may cause some additional challenges being a part of the system. Early Blu-ray players had the option of using an analog format to display content if the full digital system was unavailable. Modern players will only use High-Definition Multimedia Interface (HDMI) as the format for distributing content. While we will talk a bit more about the specifics of HDMI and other video interfaces in the next chapter, there is an important concept to understand at this juncture. Blu-ray players will use High-Definition Distribution Content Protection (HDCP). This protocol was developed in order to prevent illegal copying of high definition content. It requires all equipment, from the player to the display, to be compliant. If any piece of gear is not, the content will not be displayed. With the option of using analog signals, the designer can get by the HDCP, but the quality of the image may suffer accordingly.

HARD DISK AND SOLID STATE SYSTEMS

As more systems are dependent on computers for control and playback, the preferred method of playing content will be directly from the computer's hard drive. The hard drive will be one of a couple of different varieties, which can affect the overall performance, but will also have varying degrees of associated cost. The benefit of the drive over previous playback methods is that this method allows true random access, which is essential for interactivity and beneficial for a variety of effects. There are a number of playback systems developed by the broadcast industry (adopted for live entertainment) which are essentially specialized computers for playback, as seen below. Understanding how the drives access the data is crucial to understanding these players as well as the computer access itself.

FIGURE 6.2
Professional playback systems.

The most common drive will be the Hard Disk Drive (HDD). This is a platter based system, meaning that there is circular storage media that is spun like a record, with markers designating where a file is located. These drives can hold a tremendous amount of information—several terabytes of information on a single drive. The platter will spin at different speeds depending on the model, from 5,400 RPM to 7,200 RPM. For video systems, faster is almost always better; this is one of those times. As factors in the video increase, such as resolution and color range, file sizes will increase. While codecs are improving to compensate for larger files, the ability of the drive to quickly access the files to utilize the information may be critical. If the drive is not fast enough, playback will have a few different issues.

As a faster method of accessing information, a Solid State Drive (SSD) may be used. These drives will have considerably less storage. They are getting larger, but continue to be smaller than their mechanical counterparts. SSDs also come with a much greater price, whereas an HDD may have ten times the storage at a specific price point. On a workstation where the raw footage is being accessed to create content, this may be of concern to the designer, but not as part of the playback system. SSDs have a much greater access speed than HDDs. So, if budget allows, the SSD is preferred.

There is a third, hybrid type of drive, which combines some solid state storage in addition to the platter system. Many designers have found that this type of drive tends to wear out faster than either one of its counterparts, in the way that it is used in the entertainment industry. Obviously, individual results may vary depending on the make of the drive and how often data is written, and as technology continually improves, so may this opinion. As all drives may at some point fail, it is good to always back up all data. When an SSD fails, the information is less likely to be recoverable than for failures on an HDD.

CAMERA

While not generally used as a playback device, the camera is often used in live performance. The primary use has traditionally been for some form of image magnification (IMAG), through which the camera is capturing an image live while it is played back on a large screen. The purpose of this is generally so that those seated further from the stage are able to see a more detailed portion of the performance. Though this is often used in the music industry to highlight the lead singer or possibly a solo performance, it has been used theatrically as well. As part of the IMAG process, additional layers can be added, framing the action.

When you are using a camera in a live setting, there are a number of things to keep in mind. First of all, it is important to

FIGURE 6.3
Artistic use of IMAG—*Iris*.

Source: Matt Beard

understand that the camera does not see the world the same way as the human eye. This means that it will also adapt to changes differently than the human eye as well, especially if there is not an operator and the designer is relying on automatic settings in the camera. Cameras take in physical stimulation (light) and interpret it based on specific values set in the firmware. They do not have varying degrees of perception that the human mind may have. The designer must understand this when using a camera live, as it may require additional discussion with the lighting designer.

As a large majority of performances are designed for a proscenium styled performance, the lighting designer will light from that perspective as well. However, the media designer may not just want to have cameras in the front of house (FOH) positions. During corporate presentations or music concerts, there are often multiple cameras, some at a long distance in FOH, one or two along the side, and one or two mobile cameras to get in close to the action. Each of these camera positions will catch the light on the subject a little bit differently. The desire could be to use cameras with automatic settings in order to handle all of the changes, but this will be detrimental when using IMAG, as the color and brightness differences will be extremely obvious when switching between cameras. As there is no opportunity to correct for this in post-production, white balance will be set prior to the production, and brightness settings are set and monitored throughout the production.

As opposed to other forms of playback, latency (frame delay) is of critical concern with IMAG. Generally the greatest concern with other forms of playback is making sure that audio, if present, is played in time with the video. With forms of IMAG, the designer will also need to design a system to make sure that what is happening live will match with the video being presented. There are a number of factors which can add latency, including the amount of processing involved and the distances between equipment. The greater amount of latency, the more noticeable it will be to the audience.

STREAMING MEDIA

Many consumers are leaving broadcast television due to the preference for video on demand or other streaming media at home. However, this is not generally the best option for live performance. Essentially, streaming media is content which is stored externally to the player. If you consider the analog version of a film projector, the film stock is stored on a reel, then passed through the ether to the projector, which can display it. Older cinemas would often have a series of pulleys along the ceiling of the projection booth where the film from one projector could actually be played on two separate projectors, with the transport delay between projectors.

In the entertainment market, we can use both video on demand as well as streaming broadcast. For the most part, we use the former. When used as a reference, it can be very useful, but then it is usually not full resolution. This is often used when the media players are located near the projector, but the control hardware is located at a distance away. This way, the player can stream a preview of the file to the controller, either in a pre-visualization or as a monitoring solution. But as the player must receive the data and then decode it for playback, there is a delay in playback, plus the constant potential of lost packets, which result in buffering interruption.

COMPUTER BASED SYSTEMS

In modern systems, the computer is becoming the main source of playback. In fact it is becoming the heart of the video system, with fewer peripherals. As individual programs will vary and will evolve rapidly, we will instead focus on the main styles that can be represented that a designer may choose from. Each type of program will have its strengths, and all of them can offer challenges depending on the time available for programming and the level of flexibility desired in the design. There is a wide range in pricing, from a few hundred dollars for some programs to be installed on a computer to tens of thousands for a pre-built media server.

Slide

As some designs can be as simple as providing a simple backdrop, complex playback is not always necessary. This is similar to the idea that historical projection designers used by changing slides. Of course, as previously discussed, there was little control over the individual images. On productions such as *The Who's Tommy*, as designed by Wendall Harrington, multiple slide images could be faded in and out, creating the impression of movement. Computerized slide programs, as often used for presentations at a conference or sales meeting, are powerful enough for use in some productions.

143

The benefit for simple productions using a slide based program is that it is likely that someone in the production already has a licensed copy. These type of programs have the ability to embed videos as well as play slides. They often have a variety of transitions, such as fades and wipes, which can have theatrical effects. In addition, there is an easy method of control, either by the standard keyboard controls or by one of many commercially available wireless remotes. In addition, simple timed effects are possible.

The main drawback to this type of program is that very little manipulation of the content for playback is possible. That being said, some are available depending on how modern a version is being used. While the designer should always keep in mind what codecs can be used by the playback medium, the slide player will greatly limit the choices. The two major presentation software developers also are the authors of operating systems; thus they tend to limit codecs to the ones used by other parts of their software suites. This will only be a challenge if using stock content without the means of converting it afterwards.

Cue

A cue based software is similar to the slide based software inasmuch as it sets up playback one at a time. Similar to other cues, such as on a light console, cue based software sets up playback sequentially, but does not require one video to complete before a second begins. They grant the designer a greater freedom in the ability to control video, such as altering the speed and direction of playback. In addition, they offer an increasing amount of the types of codecs available as well.

FIGURE 6.4

Qlab is an example of cue based software.

Source: Backstage Academy

Cue based media programs work well in the traditional theatrical environment, as the productions are well rehearsed and planned to work in a specific linear fashion.

Timeline

A timeline based media program is the basis of most media servers. However, they also are available as stand-alone programs to be used on the computer of choice. This type of program may be very familiar to media designers as they resemble non-linear editors. They also offer a much greater level of control than any of the previously mentioned programs. The control options include alteration of the video through its shape and speed, and a multitude of other options. In addition, they can allow for real-time manipulation of content, not being entirely reliant on how things developed in rehearsals.

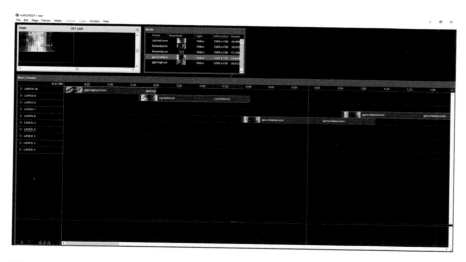

FIGURE 6.5

Watchout is an example of a timeline based program.

Source: Backstage Academy

VJ Sampling

The video jockey (VJ) is the extension of the disc jockey for live performance. At raves and dance clubs, visual entertainment set to the music has greatly advanced from strobing lights and smoke effects. VJs have come to the forefront by offering stunning media visuals. Similar to their music counterparts, they have a method of transitioning between pairs of cued media and have the skill to manipulate that media for live performance.

This may seem out of place to include with other performance media. However, these programs can be quite powerful and rather inexpensive. Many of the theatrical media servers will employ some means of sampling in combination with timelines.

FIGURE 6.6
Resolume is a powerful VJ sampling type software.

Source: Backstage Academy

Object Oriented Programming Environment

The final method of media playback is the Object Oriented Programming Environment (OOPE). This method of media control is considerably different from all others. It offers a blank slate, allowing for the method of playback and control to be designed much as the content is created. This type of software is much more geared to interactive performances as it has the greatest amount of flexibility. On the other hand, it can have an extreme learning curve as there are not the predefined effects readily available.

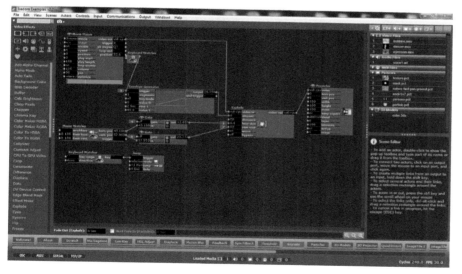

FIGURE 6.7
Isadora is an example of an OOPE.

MEDIA SERVER

The media server is the philosopher's stone for the digital alchemist. It is rapidly becoming the backbone of most modern media designs. This term loosely describes the computerized control of the media. While it can describe any computer that has media control software, stand-alone programs are not always described as such if the computer is not dedicated to that software. As we discussed in the previous section, there are a number of styles used by developers, with Timeline being the most common. A media server should have dedicated hardware to go along with the software, for optimal presentation.

FIGURE 6.8
Media server hardware—Pandora's Box.

Media control programs reside exclusively on their own hardware (generally embedded with the program and operating system). These are often desired, as the manufacturer builds the computers to work optimally with the program. For media designers, these are preferred when coming from a rental company, as content is greatly protected. Purpose-built media servers are relatively easy to reset to factory defaults, eliminating non-factory-installed content. In addition, content which is installed will be encoded with proprietary codecs which prevent copying or removal of the content.

Media servers are also becoming a popular tool for lighting designers. However, there are many who will still require the assistance of a projection designer or at the very least a video crew. The biggest challenge that lighting designers face is the distribution of the video signal. Many media servers have the ability to be controlled by the lighting console, which allows both pre-programmed shows as well as "busking", or the ability to manipulate video files live.

These are extremely powerful devices which will open up a treasure trove of possibilities as the designer has access to the budget required and the experience to use them. We will discuss more possibilities in Chapter 11 as we discuss advanced concepts in design. The measure of possibility is much beyond the ability of live compositing video, which is where newer designers will get their feet wet. As each developer has their unique means of achieving the same goals, it would be like comparing Mac OS to Linux and Microsoft, as the end result will be similar, but the devil is in the details. It is recommended to watch many training videos online to see which one to try out first.

CHAPTER 7

Distribution

In a digital system, there is the requirement to transport the source material to the display. Most often this will be a series of cables connected between them. As systems gain complexity, more specialized cables will be added, including fiber optic and wireless transmission. In addition, distribution may include re-clocking signals as well as duplicating them for multiple displays. If the display does not have the ability to use a certain signal, altering the information may be required in the distribution system.

ANALOG SUNSET

As digital media became more accessible to the consumer market, the professional market for the first time became greatly influenced by it. Generally, advances in the professional market influenced the high-end consumer market, which in turn influenced the general consumer market. As the consumer market has become digital through the transition to digital broadcast, then all equipment followed suit. This has come to be known as the "analog sunset". This has loosely been adopted by the professional audio/visual market as a preference, but was actually part of a mandate on the consumer side of things.

The Advanced Access Content System license agreement was adopted to help protect content on digital devices. It was adopted both by content providers as well as equipment manufacturers to protect Blu-ray (and previously HDDVD) content. These devices initially needed to provide for both analog and digital distribution, but as of December 31, 2013, no additional devices designed to play encrypted content may be manufactured in a way that allows for analog distribution. This was an official designation of analog sunset as part of the agreement (exhibit E, part 2, section 2.2.2).[1]

As the live entertainment market is not generally going to be playing Blu-ray content, this information is still good to know, depending on acquisition of content and method of playback. For instance, some online services, such as Apple's iTunes, which is not bound by the AACS license agreement, have provided restrictions on their downloaded content. Thus, the designer needs to know where content comes from and that there may be difficulties in playback due to distribution restrictions.

DIGITAL RIGHTS MANAGEMENT

As has been mentioned a few times, the process of protecting high definition content is through the use of digital rights management (DRM). This is a communication between the content and the entire system of display, player, and distribution to determine the ability to play back the content. If any part of the system does not comply with the HDCP standards, then the image will not appear at all or will appear as a completely static field.

For media designers, as long as there is not the desire to use media from a Blu-ray manufactured by a commercial distributor, there should be little concern over DRM interfering with a production. That being said, some equipment manufacturers who design for the consumer market will sometimes have all digital outputs looking for HDCP compliance, even if the content does not have DRM associated with it.

As most modern media designs will rely mainly on computer based systems, and royalty free content generally does not have this type of protection, DRM should be of little concern. The main point is that the designer needs to be aware of the source of the content and the method of playback so as to avoid trouble in presentation.

EXTENDED DISPLAY INFORMATION DATA

Every display has its limitations. Beyond the physical properties of the display, each one has a set of limitations as to how it can process incoming video data. Beyond the native resolution, every display will have a set of resolutions and refresh rates that it can process. Any resolution or refresh rate outside of those defined parameters will not be shown. A message of "out of range" may be displayed to let the user know that signal is reaching the display but cannot be displayed.

The EDID is a standard developed by Video Equipment Standards Association (VESA) and is a method of communication that allows the display to let the source know what its capabilities are. In older equipment, the method of starting up the connected devices could affect this communication and the order needed to be observed. A strict adherence to powering on the display prior to starting the source was necessary as the EDID was only requested at the start-up of the source. If it did not receive EDID, it would assume the worst and only display the lowest resolution used (generally VGA, or 800x600 resolution). With modern equipment, this can still be preferred (including Digital Video Interface, or DVI, handshake), but is not always necessary. For instance, when using a Windows based computer, in the display settings of a graphics card, the user can use the "detect" tab. This is the user telling the computer to request the EDID at that moment. There will now be a drop-down menu listing all available resolutions available, as well as a recommended setting which represents the display's native resolution.

As EDID is a communication between the devices, some method of information transport must be available. When using methods other than a direct connection between source and display (over copper cable), then additional means may be required. This may not be required if the display only needs EDID at start-up or if it retains the information from previous use. However, many sources need constant EDID or else they consider the display to not be there. In cases such as this, a small intermediary device may be put in line which can be programmed with the display's information and have it readily available. Figure 7.1 is a representation of such a device.

FIGURE 7.1
EDID emulator.

153

VIDEO SIGNAL INTERFACES

Over the years, there have been a number of standards as to how to deliver video. The specifics of all of them, along with their history, may be of interest to engineers, but there are some specifications which the media designer should pay attention to in order to have the best communication between components. Often, the choice of connection will be what is available on the equipment used. However, many equipment manufacturers will have multiple interface connections and knowing the limitations of each should help determine which

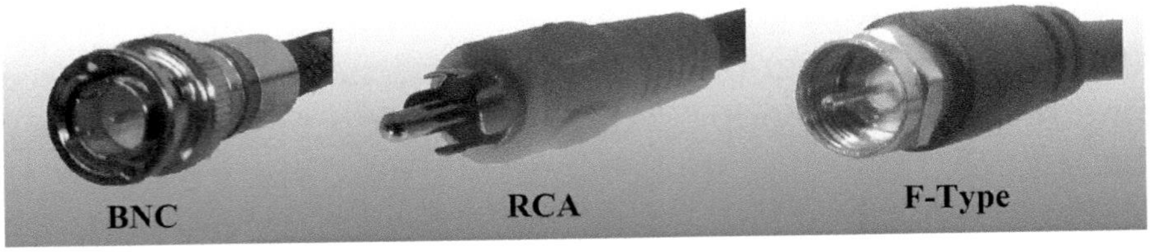

BNC   RCA   F-Type

FIGURE 7.2
Co-axial connectors.

interface to use. Some interface signals have been designed with particular connections while many older ones did not.

The first video interface, which has been known to consumers since the 1950s, is composite video, short for Composite Video with Blanking and Sync (CVBS). This interface carries the entirety of the video signal over a single 75 ohm co-axial cable, terminated most commonly with the RCA (phono) plug or a BNC (Bayonet Neill-Concelman) connector. The video transmission is limited to analog video in standard definition (480i or 576i). No audio is transmitted in this signal. This baseband signal utilizes a modulated subcarrier for the chrominance, separate from the luminance. The modulating of the composite video signal can become a broadcast channel by modulating it to a proper RF (radio frequency) carrier wave. This was common when consumer televisions did not have a composite video connection and devices would connect to the antenna through the RF connection. When that happened, audio could often be embedded in the signal as well.

The next advancement, which divided the luminance and chrominance into separate signals, was S-video. It still was an analog video for standard definition, but by separation of the two signals, it achieved a better image quality. This signal can either be carried over a pair of co-axial cables with RCA or BNC connections, or, more commonly, it is carried over a

FIGURE 7.3
S-video connector.

single cable using a mini-DIN connector. Also known as Y/C (Y=luma and C=chroma), this had limited success in the home video market due to the constraints of the VHS color system.

Continuing to build on the analog system was component video. Widely known in the consumer market by the three colored RCA connectors (red, green, and blue) on separate co-axial cables, this was the best quality picture that was available to the consumer in the analog market. This signal is now divided into three channels. The green connector carries the luminance signal as well as the synchronization. Component signals are not all the same, but modern equipment can identify the signal and make it read as needed by the display. Often a component signal is referenced as YPbPr, where Pb is the difference between blue and luma, and Pr is the difference between red and luma. Green is derived from the difference between red, blue, and the luma. As there is no multiplexing of the color information, this provided the best color representation. In addition, component allows for higher bandwidth, allowing for not only 480i, but also 480p, 720p, and 1080i.

Meanwhile, the computing industry took the signal a bit differently. The HD-15 connector, commonly known as the VGA (Video Graphics Array) connector, was the main interface connector between computers and monitors prior to the digital revolution. The standard associated with this connection

155

FIGURE 7.4
VGA connector.

utilized RGB color representation along with separate horizontal and vertical synchronization. This analog signal is sometimes sent over bundled co-axial cable as RGBS (color and sync) or RGBHV (color and separate horizontal and vertical sync). The bundled co-axial cable allows for a greater distance of transmission than the single multi-core cable with the VGA termination. This standard allowed for a greater number of resolutions and display rates.

As there was a need for higher bandwidth due to high definition digital signals, an entirely new interface was created. The Digital Video Interface (DVI) is a high bandwidth video connection utilizing the standard known as Transition Minimized Differential Signaling (TMDS) to transmit information. This

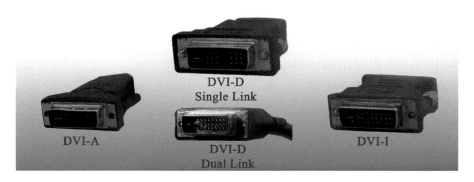

FIGURE 7.5
Sample of DVI connectors.

specification allows for the display device and the source to agree on an optimal picture size and resolution to ensure that the highest quality picture automatically happens. This is often called the "handshake" between devices. The handshake is an advanced form of the EDID and may require the start-up of the display before the source for this to happen.

DVI allows for uncompressed transmission of the video signal of up to 3840x2400 resolution on a dual-link cable. There are a variety of connectors (see Figure 7.5) which allow for lower resolutions, higher resolutions, and digital only signals, as well as the ability for analog transmission. It allows for HDCP communication, but carries no audio information. This standard was created royalty free, which helped to keep down the costs for source and display manufacturers. Many installers like the connector as it has two locking screws to maintain connectivity. Others dislike the fragility of the pins on the connector as well as the potential difficulties with the handshake if equipment is not started in the proper order. In addition, unlike analog interfaces, digital interfaces have a much shorter length of cable before signal degradation occurs. In addition, while an analog signal will get grainy, a digital signal can drop out entirely if the signal strength is too weak.

For the consumer market, the counterpart to DVI is the High-Definition Multimedia Interface (HDMI), which uses the same TMDS transmission, but adds uncompressed digital audio as well. As it is a proprietary standard, manufacturers must pay royalties to incorporate it into their equipment. The standard mandates HDCP as a means of protecting content. The rectangular connector does not lock in place and relies on compression, similar to other consumer connections. Some manufacturers, such as Apple, employed proprietary variations on digital connectors, which sometimes require adapters. Some variants did apply a rudimentary locking system, but that

FIGURE 7.6
HDMI connector.

did not necessarily work unless both parts of the connection were modified.

The broadcast industry also made the move to digital, which is borrowed by the theater industry. Serial Digital Interface (SDI) is a digital video interface used with digital grade co-axial cable and BNC terminations. There are a number of variants depending on the quality of the image and the bandwidth necessary to transport data. It can include audio of up to 16 channels, but is often used for video only. It is possible to transport high definition signals for longer distances than is possible with HDMI or DVI. However, resolutions and refresh rates are severely limited to the broadcast standards. Thus, its use in some video transmission of varying pixel ratios may not be ideal as the video is forced to be digitally altered, which adds latency and degradation of the image. However, if the entire system is SD and is maintaining a broadcast resolution such as 1080p, then this can be a very good solution.

DisplayPort is another open source standard developed by VESA. It is another high definition digital transport interface. The design of the connection is similar to that of the HDMI (compare Figure 7.6 to Figure 7.7), but it has locking tabs which make a more secure connection. Simple adapters can be used to communicate with HDMI or DVI devices, though powered adapters are required for higher definition signals.

FIGURE 7.7
DisplayPort connector and identifying symbol.

In addition, devices using DisplayPort can be daisy chained together, allowing the video card to send signals to several devices.

CABLE

The most common method of getting the video signal from the source to the display is some type of cable. These will have a variety of terminations, which may or may not be indicative of the signals they carry, as was just discussed. The type of cable will have limitations as to the amount of data that can be passed (bandwidth limitations) as well as the distance that it can pass with little to no degradation. Understanding the methods of transport is a critical method of the display infrastructure.

Copper

The most common material used in transporting data is some form of copper cable. These cables were the main method of transporting analog signals, but within the right specifications, they can properly transport digital signals as well. The standards for each of the video signal interfaces will identify the properties of the cable, including the shielding and grounding.

159

Copper cables will come in different gauges, which will affect the amount of bandwidth and distance that the cable can effectively carry the signal.

While being the most common and inexpensive method of transport, copper cables have limitations. The first issue that often arises is the limitation of distance. Most of the high definition signals end up being limited to around 9–15 feet for most communication. Some cable builds have been successful at running beyond specifications, but those cables tend to become very expensive. The other main issue that can be problematic with copper cables is electromagnetic interference. With analog signals, this can be observed as "hum bars", which are a distortion in the displayed image. Digital images can lose clarity and develop aberrations.

Adaptive Copper

Distribution lengths can often exceed the needs of standard copper cables. Even with analog signals, which allow for 100 feet or more, this is not always enough. Occasionally, having a copper cable with a greater gauge cable, one can get the length necessary if the bandwidth of the signal is low enough, but that can still be bulky and expensive. The best bet for longer runs is to adapt to a transmission system that can drive greater lengths. Often, the first choice is adaptive copper, using commonly available category unshielded twisted pair (UTP) cables such as Cat 5e.

To obtain these greater distances, the video signal will be adapted through the use of a video balun. A balun is an electronic device that transforms the video signal, which extends its range to over 330 feet. There are a great variety of these devices to match almost every variety of video signal. Baluns will sometimes be cable specific (a particular category of UTP) and others will adapt to the category of the cable. The technician will use a standard cable out of the source and connect it

FIGURE 7.8
A video balun is used to extend distance in video signal.

to the balun. Then the UTP cable will run between the sending and receiving balun, where the technician will connect another standard cable of the same type as from the source to the display. This cannot be used to switch from one type of signal to another, such as video baseband to TMDS.

Many buildings have an infrastructure of computer communication cables at patch points throughout the building. It is important that when considering the use of these patch points that the distance between patch points is known and that they are "dry lines". If the cable runs into any regular computer network system, including routers and other switches, it will not work with a standard balun. These devices do not change the signal, just the method of transportation. As soon as the signal encounters a computer protocol device, it will be rejected. Knowing the distance that is traveled in the building's infrastructure is important, as this will be added to the connections between the baluns and these patch points. Even though these signals can go much farther, there are still hard limits. If the distance is unknown, many network testers can be used to calculate the run.

One thing that can be introduced when using these devices is skew. Category cables have different twist rates between pairs of wire within the cable. This is done to reduce interference in communication in the computer system. However, this means that over long runs, it takes longer for some information to be delivered than other information. With an analog signal, this generally means that the colors arrive at different intervals, causing separation. The appearance can resemble a display out of convergence or a rainbow effect. To compensate for this, some devices will add skew correction or skew corrective devices can be added separately. If the device does not have skew correction and a separate device is not available, then skew-free cable can be used. Skew-free cable is similar in design to category cable except that all pairs are equally twisted, which prevents skewing. This cable will add to the cost over standard cables due to availability.

Fiber

Another method of increasing signal distance is through the use of optical fiber. This has the potential of obtaining extreme distances, considerably farther than any other method of transport. Similar to adaptive copper, there are a variety of cables, some which will not work with all adapters. Unlike adaptive copper, there is not one specific termination (RJ-45 for Ethernet cables). Instead, there are a variety of terminations, as well as full cable assemblies.

As different grades of fiber will have set bandwidth associated with them, some fiber adapters will use pairs or multiple pairs of fiber to transmit the signal. This will not be much of a problem for most designers as they will either rent or purchase the fiber as a package. If you are choosing to make a purchase, research will be essential to find the right package for the current production and future productions, especially with consideration for long-term use.

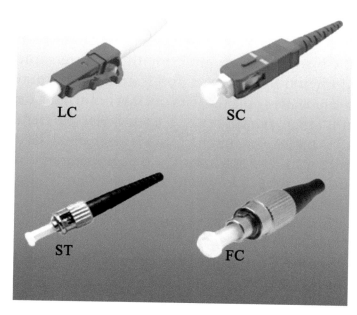

FIGURE 7.9
A sample of fiber connectors.

The biggest challenge that the projection team may encounter with the use of fiber is the transmission of EDID and making the handshake for DVI. With fiber optic adapters, EDID can sometimes be transmitted traditionally and sometimes requires a UTP line for transmission, or it can be pre-programmed into the transmitter. When using the direct method of EDID over a copper line, then the length of the run is limited by that line—usually around 330 feet. On the other hand, with virtual EDID, the fiber run can be greatly extended to a mile or more. As with other runs of DVI, the order in which units are powered up may make a difference.

Fiber can either be single mode or multi-mode. Single mode can achieve the greatest distances, but, as the name implies, traffic is a single data stream. Meanwhile, multi-mode can carry more data, but has significantly shorter effective distances (still greater than copper). As defined by ISO/IEC 11801, multi-mode fiber cable is designated by a specific optical mode (OM). The first is OM1, which is typically a 62.5 um fiber and achieves 10 Gb/s for only about 33 m, though it is more commonly used for 100 Mb Ethernet applications. OM2 uses 50 um fiber and can nearly triple the data of OM1, which makes it ideal for Gigabit Ethernet applications. Both OM1 and OM2 can work with LED based equipment. OM3 is laser-optimized 50 um fiber which can still achieve 10 Gb/s at distances of 300 m, all while handling about ten times the bandwidth of OM1. It can also be used with 40 Gigabit or 100 Gigabit Ethernet applications up to 100 m. Currently, OM4, which is also laser-optimized 50 um fiber, almost doubles the specifications of OM3, supporting 10 Gigabit Ethernet up to 550 m and 100 Gigabit up to 150 m.

Additionally, fiber cable will have colored jackets which help to identify the cable. OM1 and OM2 are typically orange. OM3 and OM4 cable usually have a jacket that is teal or aqua. When the cable is bundled for entertainment use, the outer jacket will be much more durable and will be black. Multi-mode equipment is usually more cost effective and single mode systems are often much more expensive to achieve the greater distances.

Passive/Active Adapters

There are times when the equipment available will not have all of the same methods of transmission. At that point, the cable can be adapted and possibly the signal will need to be, as well.

Passive adapters can be used when the transmission signal is of the same type. For instance, a video baseband (composite) signal may have termination with RCA or BNC. A simple adapter can be used on the cable, as there is no need to change the signal type. However, adapting a BNC cable to an F-type connector may not work, as it is likely that there is a mix of video baseband and a modulated signal. In that case, a scan converter will be required (discussed later in this chapter).

An active adapter will require power to assist in adapting the signal. These do not translate signals, as different types will still require scan converting to do so. Instead, active adapters boost the signal as they change connection types. For instance, DisplayPort is able to use TMDS as part of its protocol. This means that a DisplayPort out can be used for either a DVI or HDMI input. However, it can only use a passive adapter with a simple transmission. For high definition and refresh rate, it requires an active adapter to prevent signal loss.

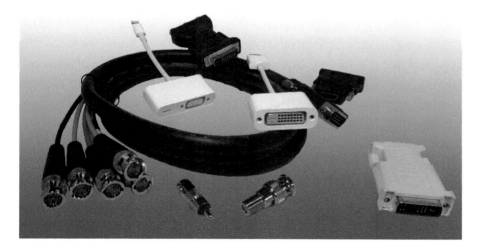

165

FIGURE 7.10
Sample adapters.

Video Over Internet Protocol
As previously mentioned, greater distance can be achieved by utilizing common Ethernet cables and baluns. Unfortunately, they cannot be connected over a network as the transmission protocols do not match. However, the video can originate or be translated to use the internet protocol (IP) as a means of

transmission. This is a popular method of closed circuit security cameras which can be used for backstage monitoring. The drawback is that the additional processing is necessary for translating the signal, which adds latency in the transmission and is not desired when used for IMAG.

While this may seem to be the ideal situation, even with systems having Gigabit speeds, other traffic on the system can bog down video. With lower definition video this will likely be just fine, but as bandwidth increases Video Over Internet Protocol (VOIP) will have difficulties if it is not a dedicated system.

HDBaseT and Audio Video Bridging

In the past few years, two more transmission protocols have been gaining traction, particularly for commercial installations but increasingly in theater as well. These also use network type cables for video. Both protocols have been established to transmit audio, video, and power over the twisted pair cables. With the intent of simplifying installations, these protocols are increasing in popularity on some shows due to their simplicity.

Introduced in 2010, HDBaseT is a standard by which manufacturers are able to transmit ultra-high definition video and audio along with Ethernet, USB, control protocols, and up to 100 w of power over a single category (Cat6 or greater) cable for up to 100 m.[2] This can not only benefit the installation by getting the increased signal length to 100 m, but it possibly also reduces the clutter of multiple cables, creating a cost savings. Since it also offers the ability to transfer power as well, this means that placing displays (there are a number of display manufacturers who have this built in) in areas where it may be difficult to add power may make this beneficial (find out more at hdbaset.org).

Meanwhile, Audio Video Bridging (AVB) is from the Institute of Electrical and Electronics Engineers (IEEE) group which set up the IEEE 802.1 technical standards.[3] In 2005, this working group had a similar idea as to what HDBaseT hopes to achieve: to develop a standard to reduce cable clutter in AV systems, all while improving them. In some ways this was the successor to IEEE 1394 (commonly known as FireWire), which was often used in post-production transportation of audio and video data. While HDBaseT was inherently designed for the consumer market (including retail installations), AVB had the intent of cross-networking between technologies that fell both within consumer products and professional gear. The benefits that it purports are improved synchronization of audio and video signals, low latency between devices, and reduction in infrastructure. They accomplish this through sub-standards, including IEEE 802.1AS (precise synchronization), IEEE 80231Qav (traffic shaping for AV streams), IEEE 802.1 Qat (admission controls), and IEEE 802.1BA (identification of participating devices). This task group continues its work as the Time-Sensitive Networking Task Group as of 2012 (learn more at www.ieee802.org).

PASSIVE SPLITTER

For many theatrical designs, we look to have the same image on multiple displays. The first basic method is the passive splitter. This will be similar to other passive adapters where there is no change to the signal. Instead of adapting from one type of connection to another, we are adapting from an individual output to multiple outputs.

Video signals, similarly to audio, are measured in decibels in regard to transmission. As they are transmitted down longer cables, adapted, or split, then they will have a loss in the energy, which degrades the signal. In order to preserve signal quality, we limit the number of interruptions between the source and the display. When you are using a passive splitter, each branch of the signal will have a known degradation of the signal. When you are designing the video system for display, planning

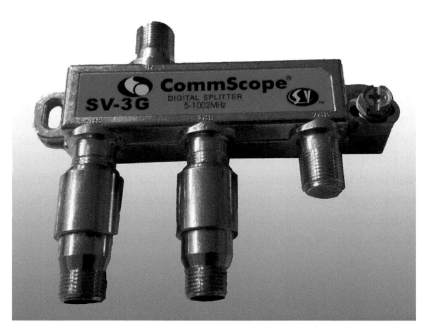

FIGURE 7.11
F-type co-axial passive splitter.

where each connection is made can make the presentation successful. By not planning where connections are made, then the designer is taking a chance on the ultimate signal strength and may risk dropouts.

DISTRIBUTION AMPLIFIER

The need to split the signal is also necessary for the operator as well. Often the video operator will not be in direct view of the display and needs a means to see what is being produced for the audience. In addition, the displays may be placed in such a way that a passive splitter may not be acceptable due to the degradation of the signal. In either case, a distribution amplifier (DA) is likely the ideal choice to divide the signal. As opposed to the passive splitter, the distribution amplifier not only splits the signal to multiple displays, but also re-clocks and boosts the signal.

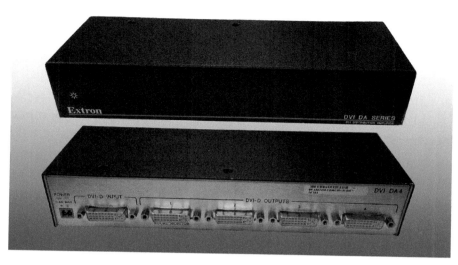

FIGURE 7.12
DVI distribution amplifier.

Typically, a DA will have a single input and then two, four, or eight outputs. The first of the outputs is designated as the local monitor (see Figure 7.12). This output will not be amplified and will be the transmission point in which the source will receive its EDID. All outputs, just like a passive splitter, will output the exact same transmission. Thus, the EDID obtained from the local monitor will be what is sent to all of the connected displays. It is important that all of the displays are compatible with the local monitor and should preferably have the same resolution and aspect ratio.

By having the local monitor not being an amplified signal, the DA is most often located near the operator. This allows for the operator to have a representation of the image visible even if he or she cannot see the end result. However, this may limit how the DA is used.

WIRELESS

It is often said that the shortest distance between two points is a straight line. When running the cables directly between the source and the display, this is rarely the case. Instead, cables are run every which way along the walls, through conduits, in cable troughs, and pretty much never the shortest distance between the two components. Keeping the cables neat and tidy adds a considerable distance, sometimes requiring some additional means of extending the cable run, but even the cost of less expensive network cables can still add up. The alternative is a wireless transmission of the signal.

A wireless bridge for video works similarly to a wireless bridge for IP communication. A transmitter will be linked to one or more receivers, though generally it is one-to-one communication. They operate in the same open frequency ranges as all other open range communications, the bandwidth that is not regulated by the FCC. Over the years, there have been great improvements in the reliability of wireless transmission, especially when keeping to broadcast resolutions. Even still, they can still be susceptible to other wireless traffic. For show critical solutions, it is best to test extensively with all systems operating at the same time, including lighting, sound, and automation. There have been many high profile events in the past that fell victim to noisy wireless communication spectrum. In addition, the FCC has been increasingly selling off the "white space" of the communication bands to mobile phone providers. Equipment may run the risk of becoming obsolete due to no longer being able to use a frequency to transmit. This has happened to wireless microphone manufacturers a couple of times.

SCALING

As has been mentioned, every display has limitations as to what video signals it can handle. This information is transmitted to the source via EDID. Generally, when the video signal comes from a computer graphics card, there will not be issues, as the computer has a wide range of display capabilities. When using video hardware that has a limited range, such as optical disk or magnetic tape based systems, we often must alter the signal before it is ultimately displayed. The first method is scaling, which refers to the resolution of the image and changing the effective resolution. Modern displays have the ability to process the image, such as an HDTV converting a signal from a DVD player, but external processing is often many times more powerful and may result in less latency or greater image quality.

With an analog signal, the scaler will additionally adjust the clocking and phasing of a video signal (auto adjustment on a

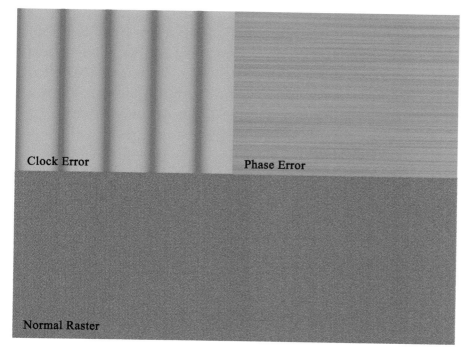

FIGURE 7.13
Clocking and phasing correction in analog signal.

display will handle this). A digital signal will have the clocking and phasing as part of the EDID, simplifying the process and often making a scaler unnecessary for modern displays. Scalers will also provide blanking abilities, which allow the user to crop the edges which may exceed the display area. Rarely would it be necessary to use a dedicated scaler in a video system today. This is more often just part of another piece of equipment, which will be discussed in Chapter 8.

SCAN CONVERTING

Although we use the term "video" universally for visual display signals, the way the signals are transmitted and created are actually different. Similar to a modulated frequency and a baseband video signal that require translation—the baseband video being shown on the AV input with the modulated frequency being a channel on a television—a computer signal will also vary from the baseband video signal. Simple scan conversion was used in the early days of personal computers being connected to CRT monitors. Like scalers, most modern scan converters are part of switchers and mixers. This allows the designer the flexibility of sending multiple types of inputs to the display without switching inputs on the display.

RESOLUTION MULTIPLIER

Often a designer will be looking to multiply the surfaces which can carry an image or otherwise stretch the capacity of the design. Budget does not always allow for multiple computers or the ability to keep them all synchronized. In this case, the designer can employ a resolution multiplier. This device will provide a different EDID than the display device. It will allow for two or three times the width of a typical display. The computer's graphics card will see this as an extremely wide display, but this will allow the designer to use that single output to be distributed to multiple displays having the same or different content. These do require all of the displays to have the identical resolution, but this can be a minor trade-off for the added flexibility.

FIGURE 7.14
Example of a resolution multiplier.

NOTES

1. Advanced Access Content System ("AACS") Adopter Agreement, June 19, 2009
2. hdbaset.org
3. www.ieee802.org

CHAPTER 8

Control

All media designs will require some method of control. This control may require an operator or it may be completely automated. In this chapter we will discuss a wide variety of methods which will be essential tools as the designs become more complicated. These tools have been adopted from the broadcast industry as well as installed audio visual systems. Many of these tools have been incorporated into modern media servers, though the concepts remain the same. As with other technology we have discussed, sometimes there are different methods to implement the same concept.

SWITCHERS

As was mentioned with scan converting, the designer may require multiple playback devices to be sent to a single display. Even when using a media server, the designer may choose to use a switcher when incorporating IMAG as a method to minimize latency. A switcher is a device which allows multiple sources to be connected to a single display, letting the user select which source is seen at any given time. There are two main differences between these devices; they are either passive or active in the way that they deal with the video signals.

Passive

Rarely used in live performance, the passive switcher will be the least expensive option. Similar to passive adapters, there is no processing of the video signal in these devices. Due to the lack of processing, they require all of the same type of video signal. By using this type of switching device, the designer depends on the video processing of the display to handle any scan conversion and scaling required. As such, when switching between one source and another, the display may have visual glitching such as flashes or digital artifacts. In other words, it is best that the audience cannot see the displayed image while switching occurs.

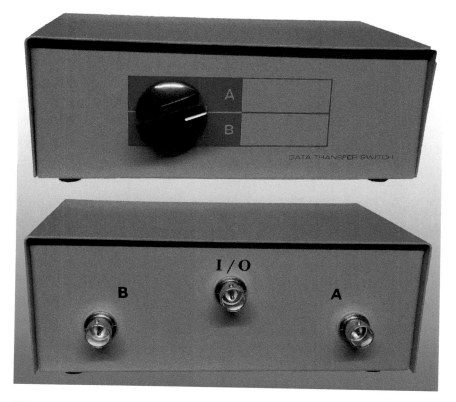

FIGURE 8.1
Example of a passive switcher.

Active

As the presentation of the image is just as critical as what the image represents, having the image glitch as switching occurs between inputs is less than desired. Switchers that offer the ability to change without noticeable error at the display require video processing. There are two types of active switcher: the most basic glitch-free and the more advanced seamless switcher.

Glitch-Free/Presentation

Because designers do not want the audience to see visual distractions when switching from one source to another, glitch-free switchers generally offer scaling and scan converting in order to send one unified signal to the display. Ideally, this signal is set to its native resolution, allowing the display to provide the best image. This processing ability greatly increases the cost of the device over a passive version. However, with the ability to convert the image, this offers the designer more flexibility in the display, as this type of switcher often offers many different outputs, both analog and digital, and broadcast and computer waveforms. All of the outputs are live at the same time (providing that the signal is compatible with that output). This allows the operator to sometimes use a secondary output to see what is being currently sent to the display on a monitor backstage. This can be used either if the operator is out of view of the display or as a confidence monitor that the signal is good to that point.

The glitch that occurs in the display from a passive switch is the processing needed to calibrate the new signal. Higher end displays can save the input settings of the source, which makes the process quicker. The issue at hand is that while switching from one source to another, the video processor needs to find the start of the video signal. The glitch-free switcher will either display a period of video black or use a saved image to transition between signals in order to establish the start of the video signal before presentation of the new image. This can

FIGURE 8.2
Example of a glitch-free switcher.

take as little as one second. While this switcher is common in meeting spaces, the transition time is not always acceptable for the live entertainment market. As presentation switchers only have one video processor, there is no way to speed this up. The switch ejects the current signal and then processes the new signal during the period of black or stored image display.

177

Seamless

The addition of a second video processor to the device can offer truly seamless switching. While the glitch-free processing can allow for cross fades through black or a saved still image, the seamless switcher can allow for cross fades between images to some degree. Depending on the ability of the processor, it may freeze the outgoing video to a still image while the new video fades in. Dual-processor switchers will often offer additional broadcast style switching methods besides the cut and fade. While these may not fit within most theatrical designs, the additional processing power may still be desired. Since it allows for observing a preview signal, there is an additional step in the transition, known as "take". This is the step which executes the switch between signals based on the preview selected and the type of transition selected.

The seamless switcher is able to fade between video signals because the secondary processor provides a preview of the next source. This means that the switcher is already processing the next signal before the change, while the glitch-free processor does not have the ability to process the new signal until the switching process begins. This can limit the variety of outputs that the device will have (generally fewer types than the glitch-free switcher).

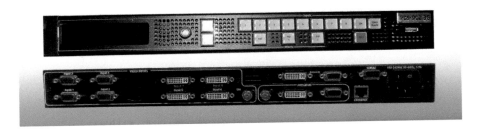

FIGURE 8.3
Example of a seamless switcher.

Beyond the ability to transition seamlessly between video signals in front of the audience, these switchers give the operator confidence in being ready for their next cue. By offering the ability to preview the signal before it is sent, the operator knows if any problems have developed. With other forms of switching, the operator will need to split each input and have a monitor for each source to preview it before switching. This may be worth the additional expense on its own.

MIXERS

Those who have seen the original *Star Wars* movie have already seen large mixers in action, except that they were repurposed to operate the planet destroying weapon. Generally designed with the broadcast industry in mind, a mixer is similar to the seamless switcher, sometimes without scan converting ability (sticking to one type of signal) but with additional transitions.

The mixer is ideal when transitioning between cameras, as they are running the same type of signal. Without the need of providing scan converting, cross fades can usually occur without freezing the outgoing image. As with all other equipment, there are a range of mixers with a very large range of pricing.

The more basic mixers are all in one device. They have a control surface which allows the operator to choose between inputs, the type of transition, and the method of transition. With the seamless switcher, the operator would press the take button to execute the switch. But with a mixer, the operator also has a T-handle to execute the switch manually at their own fade rate (as opposed to the programmed rate of the take button).

179

FIGURE 8.4
Example of a mixer.

Large mixers (like the prop on the Death Star) are actually just control surfaces. The processing of the signals and their subsequent distribution is actually taking place in additional processing units. These could be combined with other stand-alone devices, but most manufacturers find that dedicated modules offer the best product. As opposed to the all-in-one devices, the large mixers provide the operator with the ability to program the control surface in order to fit the needs of the production. They also can provide the operator with control over multiple outputs at the same time, allowing for much more advanced designs.

MATRIX ROUTERS

Media designs are not limited to an individual display or image. A design may incorporate many different displays, all of which may require the same image or different images simultaneously. Instead of using a complex maze of splitters and switchers, a matrix router can be used. This allows for many inputs to be diverted to a number of outputs. Routers do not process the signal, but simply direct the signal to the appropriate display.

FIGURE 8.5
Example of a matrix router.

Routers are most often designed with the same number of inputs as outputs. They are often used in conjunction with a separate control surface, including the previously mentioned mixers. However, they can have a very simple rack mounted control surface consisting of a row of buttons representing each input and another row for the outputs, with the addition of the take button. Routers that are the processing units for mixers will be much more complicated units which can offer some signal processing that older units could not. As with everything discussed before this, the more options that a designer is looking for, the greater the price of the equipment.

COMPUTERS

Going beyond the complex computing power that goes on in all of the previously mentioned devices, including the processing in the displays, many designers will be relying on the personal computer. Media servers, as discussed in Chapter 6, are either self-contained or are contained in a program on a computer. They are already a controlling element of the media system. Beyond manipulating the image to one or more displays, they

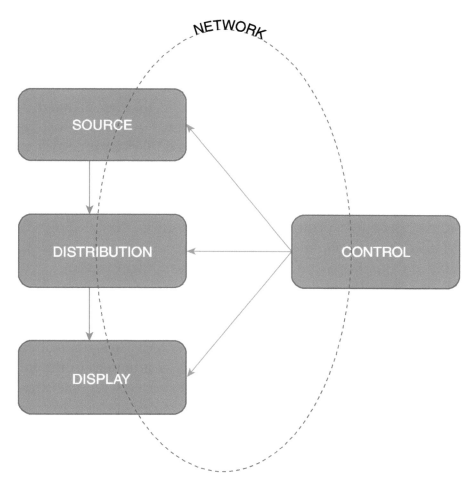

181

FIGURE 8.6
Component relations of a media system.

can send out a variety of control protocols to tell other equipment what to do, simplifying the operation to a central unit. They can create an automated system, spouting out commands too complicated for an individual operator to replicate. As more devices are network compatible, computers are essential for monitoring specific equipment and directing components to work with one another. They become the critical component of the five-piece puzzle that is the media system.

CONTROL COMMUNICATION

It would be wonderful to say that the designer had to understand a single, universal protocol for control communication. Of course, that would be too easy. Not only that, it probably would not be theatrical (though we have tried). After all, the entertainment industry develops little on its own; instead, it borrows, adapts, and emulates what it finds in other industries in order to find new ways to make magic. When it comes to media systems, the adaptability also comes into play when working with departments that are much more established, and working with the controls established with them. Of the following control protocols, the bulk of the understanding will be needed by designers choosing to use media servers. After all, they are a main part of the overall show control system.

Timecode

In large productions, which are built to last years and require precision between multiple technical elements, designers often have relied upon timecode. Now, this is a generic term for numeric codes which are generated in sequence at regular intervals in order to synchronize a number of devices in a system. Video editors will likely be familiar with the Society of Motion Picture and Television Engineers (SMPTE) timecode, which is used for the synchronization of multiple elements when editing. There are a variety of different formats, but media design is primarily concerned with only a couple of them.

The main use of timecodes will be to sync audio and video. The two primary timecodes that are used between the systems are Linear Timecode (LTC) and Vertical Interval Timecode (VITC). The former is embedded in an audio track while the latter is encoded in a scanline of a video signal (generally part of the vertical blanking interval). As video can be interlaced, the VITC can actually be presented twice per frame. While these timecodes can be used beyond editing, productions will more commonly use MIDI Timecode (MTC).

All timecodes are represented in units of hours, minutes, seconds, and frames. MTC allows for drop frames (29.97 fps) for NTSC video. In addition, it can handle 24, 25, or 30 fps. Each component is encoded as straight binary, while other forms of timecode use a binary-coded decimal. MTC uses system exclusive (SysEx) messages, which are more thorough messages than standard MIDI, due to being able to be proprietary to a specific manufacturer, allowing for triggering of specific devices. Sometimes this comes as a SysEx ID, where two of the same devices can be triggered separately by their unique ID.

MIDI

So, what is MIDI? The Musical Instrument Digital Interface is a technical standard which has been used since the early 1980s as a means to interface between computers, electronic musical instruments, and other related devices. It was devised as a means for professional musicians and producers to control a variety of components to create digital music. It was specifically designed as a control protocol for the music industry and is still an effective means, as many digital audio workstations are still designed specifically to have MIDI as an integral component.

While MIDI can be an absolutely fascinating subject, including how it was originally intended to be used and the developments for the music industry, this is not really why it is included here for the media designer. It has been adopted by the entertainment industry as a control protocol for many other applications, such as MTC. MIDI commands are able to be used to directly control stage lighting and are often used by many media servers to trigger cues.

While the music industry uses a 5-pin DIN connector, there are common adapters which allow MIDI to connect via USB or Ethernet for communicating with computer programs. Each of the 5-pin connectors is designed for unidirectional communication. Generally, only three of the five pins are used, these being a ground wire and two balanced pair connectors for a 5 v signal. If multiple MIDI devices are used, then an opto-isolator should be used to electrically separate and prevent ground loops. As MIDI devices can be susceptible to interference, the cable length is usually kept to less than 50 feet. This reduces the possibility of errors as there is no inherent error detection in the protocol. A device will have up to three ports: an in port, an out port, and possibly a thru port. All of the connections on the device will be female, while the cables will all be male plugs. When the USB adapter is used, it will have two tails: an in and an out. The in goes to the out of the device, while the out goes to the in of the device. If there is no out port on a device, then that device does not have the ability to generate data. The thru port (if present) will allow devices to be daisy chained, as the device will create a copy of all data received on the in port (which adds delay). To avoid delay in the control system, a MIDI thru box can be employed, acting as a DA and sending out all of the re-clocked data together.

While the media designer will likely be using a media server to control other devices, as often seems to be the simplest manner of show control, this may not be practical. Lighting control desks often contain MIDI ports, though not all of them can be set up for more than rudimentary controls. More often, it will be the audio department that is using a MIDI controller. Some type of two-octave, piano style keyboard is the most common controller. As seen in the DJ market, specialized controllers with programmable buttons are also used.

There is a new standard of MIDI which has been in discussion for years. It should offer full backwards compatibility, and should offer higher speed transmission of data. It should also offer benefits such as plug-and-play device discovery and enumeration. Of course, it also promises a greater data range. Proposed transports even include AVB.

OSC

Similar to MIDI is another protocol which is becoming widely adopted, the Open Sound Control (OSC). OSC also networks digital musical instruments with computers, and it was also specifically developed to include multimedia devices for the purpose of show control. As opposed to the specific 5-pin DIN connector or various adapters, OSC was designed to use Ethernet cables and use internet protocols. It is a product of the UC Berkeley Center for New Music and Audio Technology (CNMAT) and is a subject of ongoing research. As such, it is often embraced by designers who love to experiment with content and control. Developer resources and much more information on the developments can be found on their website at opensoundcontrol.org.

Encoders

As we get further into the development of media design, we often work in a much more automated world. In some cases, this is literally true. Projected elements can actually move with automated scenery. In Chapter 11, we will get into detail about all of the techniques that can be employed along with encoding devices. For now, let us look at what they are.

Encoders are devices which electronically monitor the position of a device through mechanical motion. They are able to provide motion control systems with the data concerning position, speed, and direction. There are a variety of methods that can be used to create this data. These include absolute and incremental encoders, which can be optical, mechanical, or magnetic. These devices are used to precisely measure the movement of a device. When an automated set piece on a large production is moved, the automation department often needs to know the exact measurement of where the device is for the aesthetics of the production, in addition to the safety of the working environment.

Optical incremental rotary encoders have a transparent disc with equally spaced, opaque sections which are used to determine movement. An LED passes light through the disk to be detected by a photo detector. It measures pulses per revolution, providing the information about position, and can be used to determine speed. This type of device must be homed for accurate measurement, as any loss of data can give false readings unless it has an accurate index channel.

Absolute encoders are more accurate, as they are less susceptible to interference and misreads. The optical absolute encoder also uses the LED and photodetector, but uses a stationary mask which corresponds to a unique position as the light is detected as code. As this data is unique throughout the revolution of the device, exact positioning can be determined.

There are also magnetic rotary encoders which avoid the three vulnerabilities of their optical counterparts. Optical encoders can have seal failures which permit the entry of contaminants, the optical disk can shatter, and they can have bearing failures. Any of these can render them useless. The first two vulnerabilities are completely avoidable with magnetic rotary encoders, while their mechanical design makes the third less likely.

Beyond those basic encoders, there is also a linear encoder, which is a reading head linked to a scale. The sensor reads the scale to convert the position into a signal which is transformed to a digital readout. Movement is determined by the changes in position as determined by time. This method is used with both optical and magnetic linear encoders. The optical encoders are similar to the rotary encoders; they pass light through a series of openings to measure movement using a grating pitch. A separate referencing opening is used to give it precision. Meanwhile, the magnetic sensor for a linear encoder system detects the change in the magnetic field along a scale. This system is better for harsh environments where encoders could get interference from light, oil, or debris such as dust.

Finally, there is the commutation encoder, which uses the same fundamental components as the incremental encoder but adds a commutation track along the outer edge of the disk. As the LED passes through the glass disk, it pulses. The output is measured in pulses per revolution, which are used to determine the position or speed. Then the outer part of the disk provides the controller with the information on the exact position of the motor poles through information on the commutation track. This allows the controller to provide efficient power to the motor.

It may be useful for the designer to work with the automation department to understand what types of encoders are being employed with various set pieces. This will allow him or her to determine the type of data to be retrieved from the encoders as it pertains to the media system. As can be seen, there are various levels of accuracy among encoders. This may or may not influence the decision in how they will be used.

Serial Communication

Before internet protocols became one of the most prevalent forms of networking devices for means of control and feedback, serial communication was the dominant means of doing so. Serial communication is the process of sending data a single bit at a time in sequence. It is useful for long distance communication between devices where other communication may be impractical. Serial communication offers improved signal integrity, in part due to the bit by bit transmission.

Most often, serial communication is referring to the RS232 port, which uses a 9-pin (DB9) cable. This type of serial cable, unlike most video cables, will terminate one side male and the other side female. That same serial port was often used by other standards, such as RS422 and RS485, which allowed control over several devices at once. Occasionally the communication needed to swap pins as different protocols were used, requiring a null modem adapter. Though RS232 has fallen out of favor, there are several variants of serial communication using a serial stream of data (including Ethernet, USB, DMX512, and MIDI) as opposed to parallel data; these are very popular in the entertainment industry.

Serial communication was originally designed to connect two integrated circuits on the same circuit board. In order to reduce the number of pins on an integrated circuit (and reduce cost), they would use a serial bus to transfer data when speed was not an issue. Serial communication transfers less data per clock cycle than parallel communication, but does so more accurately. However, there are ways around this to speed it up, including asynchronous serial communications.

Virtual Network Computing

As a graphical desktop sharing system, Virtual Network Computing (VNC) is a means where one computer is able to remotely control another computer. In order to do this, the keyboard and mouse movements are transmitted from one computer to another. There are a number of variants (as VNC is technically the trademark of RealVNC Ltd.), some of which are open source, while others are not. Some variations include file sharing while others are optimized for a specific operating system. Each variant will have a different method of dealing with the bandwidth requirements for the control protocol.

While most of us may be used to something like Windows Remote Desktop protocol, where a friend or help desk can remotely control a computer for a fix, the pixel data for VNC is more rudimentary. VNC sends raw data, but has the ability to control a wider range of computers. Protocols like Remote Desktop are more specialized and can better display the graphic layout of the controlled computer.

There are numerous applications where this could be used in entertainment. One of the most common uses is for keeping the operator in front of house, but having the source computer closer to the display. That way, the distance of distribution is minimized, preventing the use of additional hardware to extend the signal.

189

Art-Net/Ethernet

As a popular communication protocol for the entertainment lighting industry, Art-Net is also a popular control protocol for many different media servers as well. Art-Net is an Ethernet protocol developed by Artistic License. The communication system was developed for the DMX512 standard and can control many different universes within that protocol. It was developed shortly after DMX512-A was ratified, thus expanding as manufacturers implemented that protocol in all of their lighting products. It was an open source protocol, allowing it to be used royalty free by manufacturers.

Jumping into the modern production era, with the ever growing demand for control of more channels, the current version of Art-Net is Art-Net 3. This maintains the compatibility with older systems, but can now handle up to 16,000,000 channels. That may seem like an extensive amount of channels that could never be used, but then again, people had felt that 500 lumens might have been all that was needed for digital projectors. With all of the parameters potentially able to be controlled, a single media server can start eating up the channels for control very rapidly.

Digital Multiplex

So, that brings us to the DMX protocol. As digital lighting advanced, every manufacturer was looking to control their systems. It became clear that they needed to work together. As stated, DMX is a serial protocol. It was based on RS485. The input/output is easily identified by connection to a 5-pin XLR cable. As often only three of the five pins are used, some manufacturers will use 3-pin XLR cables as well (which is outside the standard). Since that matches up with common audio cables, there has been the tendency for many low budget productions to use the same cables. Unfortunately, over long runs, this can cause errors as the standards between microphone cables and digital lighting cables are not compatible.

The standard has undergone a number of revisions. It was first ratified in 1990 and was followed by DMX512-A in 1998 (developed by USITT, the United States Institute for Theatre Technology, and maintained by ESTA, the Entertainment Services and Technology Association). It was then made an ANSI standard in 2004 (ANSI E1.11-2004). It was last revised in 2008. As it is based on a serial protocol, it can also be transmitted over UTP.

Why 512? That is the number of channels within a single universe to be controlled by this standard. When using XLR cables, each universe requires its own output. This can be extremely limiting, so most communication is transferred over Ethernet cables. The transmission of the signal is a sequential packet. These packets are repeatedly transmitted for the robustness of the signal. The controller can send these packets at different rates, which need to be uniform between devices for better results. As the DMX signal is broadcast, multiple units can listen and respond to commands. Devices which have multiple channels of control are set to the first channel to be controlled. The programmer then skips the appropriate number of channels before assigning the next fixture.

While DMX was designed for controlling theatrical lighting systems, it has become increasingly present in many media systems as well. As stated earlier, many media designs increasingly become a part of the lighting department. In the rental/staging business, which produces many large-budget, spectacular shows, the use of projectors as digital lighting tools is becoming more prevalent. In order to have their products work with these systems, projector manufacturers have included DMX protocol as a means of control of several systems within the projector. Large venue projectors often have internal shutters to block the unwanted light of video black. DMX control allows the lighting designer to operate the shutter, which is extremely important during a blackout. There are any number of controls that this may operate, such as input choice and powering the projector on or off.

Controller Interface Transport Protocol

Controller Interface Transport Protocol (CITP) is a means by which lighting controllers, media servers, and visualizers are able to transport non-show critical information during pre-production. This protocol was designed to make sure that products from different manufacturers were able to communicate between lighting consoles and visualizers. Similar to other protocols such as Art-Net, this is a means by which to establish bi-directional communication for equipment of differing operational protocols. This has been implemented in a variety of media server programs as well as some lighting systems. It is intended to be used during pre-production as it is not a real-time protocol.

Media Server Extensions Layer

The Media Server Extensions Layer (MSEX) protocol is managed by the same company as CITP and allows for specific elements to be transformed between media servers and lighting consoles. These elements currently include media, cues, effects, cross fades, masks, and presets for blend, effects, and the image. It is designed to use DMX channels for the media library and control of the media file (thus up to 256 libraries, each containing up to 256 files). Limited consoles, media servers, and visualizers are currently enabled to use this protocol, which will need to be researched by the designer should this be a desired type of control.

Syphon/Spout

Media servers and other media control programs are amazing tools, but there is the occasion when the media designer does not have all the right tools in the same package. Sometimes the designer may need two different programs to be able to share video elements. To do this, the designer may employ Syphon (for Mac) and Spout (for Windows) to allow frame sharing between applications. This can allow for videos to be shared to platforms that normally do not have interoperability, as well as the ability to use resources from separate programs to enhance the visuals.

NETWORK

The final portion of the media design is the network of the systems. This will serve as a means of communication between all of the devices. As we have discussed, several control protocols can use the network to deliver their messages. Also, the operator can use the network to get data about attached devices, such as the status of a projector. When the designer is setting up complex projection displays, the network can provide access that is unavailable or unwieldly when using wireless (or wired) remote controls. The network is based on computer system protocols and utilizes the equipment for that industry as well.

Internet Protocol

The internet protocol (IP) is the principal communications protocol for digital message formats for exchanging messages between computers across a network (single or interconnected). Messages are transferred via datagrams known as packets. The main task of an internet protocol is to deliver the packets from the host (source computer) to its destination (receiving computer) based on an address. The address information is part of the metadata, and the internet protocol includes a method of putting tags, along with the data, through a process called encapsulation. Currently there are two versions of IP that are being used: IPv4 and IPv6. For most local networks, IPv4 will be used, especially as some of our network systems were derived before IPv6 and cannot be upgraded.

Addressing and routing are the most challenging aspects to those who are unfamiliar with establishing a network. If you do not understand the basics of addressing and how the network is managed, this will prevent data transfer. Addressing works similar to a postal address that gives the house number, city, state, and other pertinent information. With IP, the address is divided into networks and subnetworks. The addressing on IPv4 will consist of four octets, which are divided by a decimal point. This is known as a quad-dotted address. This address is divided into two parts: the network identifier and the host identifier. In addition to the IP address is the Subnet Mask, which had to be implemented in computer networks because

193

the 256 network identifiers was inadequate for many installations. There are a couple of private network schemes that were set aside by the Internet Assigned Numbers Authority and are unrestricted for this purpose. These are designated as 10.0.0.0, 172.16.0.0, and 192.168.0.0, with the first being able to host the greatest number of addresses. The packets within these addresses are not routable in the public internet and are ignored by all public routers. IPv6 adds two additional octets, which became a necessity with so many devices being continually connected to the internet. As entertainment networks are not that large, IPv4 will probably be continually used until that protocol is phased out entirely.

Switches and Routers

Just as the media system in most productions develops past a single source and display, the amount of communication between devices is also in need of direction. For our networking purposes, we choose to not reinvent the wheel and instead directly use equipment designed for the computing industry. Network switches and routers are highly effective tools for getting our IP signals quickly and efficiently to the right equipment.

The network switch allows multiple devices through the use of packet switching to receive, process, and forward data between the host and receiving device. This is a more sophisticated bit of hardware that is able to send the data only to the devices that need to receive it. It is more advanced than a network hub, which only broadcasts data—this can slow down a network by delivering data to devices that do not need it, eating up precious bandwidth. In addition, switches can be managed, allowing them to work on multiple networks and keeping traffic separate that could cause equipment to get "confused".

A switch that runs on a third layer of interoperability is often referred to as a router. This is a networking device that has the ability to forward the data packets between computer networks. Thus, routers have the ability to allow communication between a private network and the internet. This has successfully allowed some events to provide users on the internet to send commands to alter visual designs and see the results live over a webcam.

Wireless Bridging

As with other parts of an entertainment network, getting a signal from point A to point B over wired transmission can become problematic. Distances between the points may be close enough for direct communication, but due to the need to keep the data lines out of the way of the audience, distances for going around it may exceed the normal specifications. In addition, the connected devices may be on non-stationary platforms. For instance, a controlled display may be on a moving set piece, which prevents any wired devices to be connected. Regardless of the reason that direct communication over network cable is not possible, a wireless bridge is often employed.

195

A simple bridge connects two network segments. Essentially, it is the crossing guard between wired segments. It will store and forward information to ensure that frame integrity is verified (it makes sure the pedestrian gets across safely). Similar to a switch, it only forwards the frames that are required to cross.

A multiport bridge is more similar to a network switch in that it is responsible for multiple connections and directs traffic to one or more recipients. It also typically stores and forwards the traffic to make sure that it successfully makes the jump over the wireless gap.

System Management

When we are only connecting a few devices using IP, then there are likely to be few problems, if any. As the systems grow, a network management system needs to be put in place. This is a set of hardware or software tools that allow the network manager to supervise individual components within a specified framework. This will allow for discovering and identifying devices that are on the network. It will monitor the devices to determine the overall health of network components and the extent to which they are performing according to capacity plans. It will track certain performance indicators such as the bandwidth utilization, latency, packet loss, and the uptime of routers and switches. An information technology professional can configure alerts to allow the user to understand challenges within the system.

Data Transfer and File Sharing

When a media designer is taking on all of the responsibilities of the design team, he or she will likely have everything stored on one single computer. As the design team grows, data files will need to be shared among several individuals. If the team members are all in the same room, it is possible to put the information on a portable drive and hand it to the next person. However, even when people are in the same room, this may not be the best option. Since we have already discussed the need for a network, let us look at another scenario.

A production could potentially have the media programmer/operator in the front of house, especially during tech week. If the show happens to be using media servers along with a video wall or rear projection, then the servers will be located backstage near the display devices. The designer is working with the programmer and has some changes to the content. The programmer is making changes to the current scene, but the designer wants this new content available as soon as the programmer is done. Instead of loading everything to a portable drive and taking the time to walk to the servers and load the content, they will have the ability to push the files over the network.

Computer operating systems often have built-in file sharing systems designed for a Local Area Network (LAN). This is easiest if both computers are running the same operating systems. Media server control platforms will also have their own method of doing this, instead of using an option like a homegroup built into the OS. As media files can be quite large, this may take too much time if the network is not designed for this. The network should be running on at least a one Gigabit switch for this to be effective.

If the design team is separated and not on a single LAN, then the file sharing is often being done over the internet. An older method, which is generally too slow for media files, is known as the file transfer protocol (FTP). This used a dedicated server to which a client would log in to obtain copies of the files. Email servers often do not allow for the transfer of files as large as many media files. There are numerous cloud based web services which allow the designer to upload a file, only sharing that file with users who are given a unique identifier to download that content. This may present some security issues, which may or may not cause the designer to look for other options.

Information Preservation
Not every production is a one-off. Many shows in a corporate theater environment can run for decades. The information regarding the show needs to be preserved. Most of us have suffered the loss of a hard drive at some point in our personal or professional careers. This can be particularly frustrating during the creation of a show. This is why we back up our data often and this should be a part of every designer's workflow. As we network our workspaces, this can be simplified.

As the design team and productions grow, the data preservation can become more difficult. So, the designer should have a detailed plan for the preservation of the information (media files and associated design paperwork) from its creation through the archive process. This will need to be worked into the budget to purchase drives (or optical disks if desired), cloud storage, or whatever method is necessary to prevent the costs associated with data loss. Make sure that there is appropriate metadata with all files so that they can be accessed and utilized by others. Have multiple copies, potentially by storing the information with multiple means (both local and cloud storage). Understand the time necessary for file transfers. When archiving, understand that file formats and technologies change, so have a plan to update if necessary (consider how few computers even have optical drives). Include in the plan who will manage archives to ensure that the data is properly managed. Plan for the security of the storage (that free online cloud storage is probably not the most secure, as several celebrities found out). Finally, do not forget about the copyrights of all of your data. If the design does not include all original material, then consider the ramifications to the long-term storage and potential use by others who may not be part of the initial design team (for example, when remounting a show). This is all part of good stewardship.

CHAPTER 9

Presentation

The most important aspect of the design is how it eventually looks. Up to this point, we have been preparing for the presentation. Now is the time to implement these ideas. Presentation challenges with most displays have been discussed along with the description of those displays. However, when you are using projectors, additional considerations need to be addressed. The amount of detail required, as described in this chapter, will have a lot to do with the content. When presenting still images or relatively small text, optical precision is much more important than it is for content with continual motion or less identifiable subjects. This is why we encourage the understanding of human perception and which details will be noticeable.

OPTICAL ALIGNMENT

Designs using projectors can offer unique challenges. Ideally, as in a cinema, the projector will be just above the audience, perpendicular to the screen, with the lowest angle of incidence possible. This is often not possible and several factors will come in to play. If the projector is placed off axis, meaning that it is not perfectly perpendicular to the projection surface, it will develop a keystone image. Images that do not fit the surface will require the projector to be placed closer or farther away for a fixed lens, or will require the use of a zoom lens, which changes the plane of projection through additional manipulation of the light in the lens assembly.

In addition to the potential for having the projection off axis, there is the very real possibility of not having a flat projection, or the surface may be irregularly shaped. This presents the designer with the challenge of digitally altering the image. With the large venue projectors used in the biggest shows, a lot of image processing is built into the projector. However, for the majority of the projectors made, very little image correction is available because the projectors are made for traditional settings. In this case, and even in the case of large venue projectors, applying image correction on the front end is required.

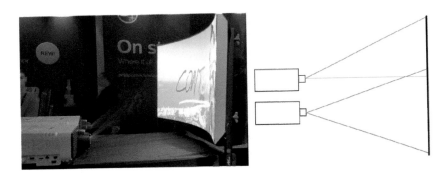

FIGURE 9.1
Angle of image projection.

Finding the optimal position for the projector requires understanding how the lenses are fashioned. On large venue projectors, the light emanating from the lens will be similar to that of a flashlight, at equal angles from the center axis. As the image is rectangular, the horizontal and vertical angles are different. However, with boardroom and home theater style projectors, this image is projected differently. Instead of equal angles, the vertical image projection will have a very shallow angle towards the bottom of the projector, while having a strong angle towards the top of the projector. This is designed with the intent that the projector will be on a table, placed low enough to not be a viewer obstruction, or it will be mounted above the screen, for the same reason. The issue that comes in is that if a projector is above the screen, but not inverted, this will result in a greatly keystoned image. To eliminate this, the projector's processor will be able to flip the image vertically, allowing the projector to be mounted upside down. This allows the optical image to be projected as intended.

With large venue projectors, placement is often less than ideal. As they are very large, they will often not be placed in the optical center. As long as the projector is still perpendicular to the screen, the image can often be moved through lens shift. The lens mount on these projectors is not permanently fixed, but is on slides which shift position with small motors. As the image is no longer projected through the center of the lens, its angles will no longer be equal. Instead, they become similar to the home theater projector—on the vertical as well as the horizontal. This will maintain the shape of the image, though the brightness will diminish slightly, often imperceptibly. Beyond adjusting the position of the image for the surface, lens shift will play an important part in advanced projection with multiple projectors.

KEYSTONE CORRECTION

The simplest image correction, which is part of almost all modern projectors, is fixing keystone. When the projector is off axis, often above or below the screen, the image from the projector spreads out, creating a larger image further from the projector. In order to correct this physical effect, the image needs to be digitally corrected. The image processor, whether part of the projector or an external device, will take the expanded portion of the image, blank out the unwanted lighted area, and compress the image to the new area. However, the physical limitations of the projector have not changed; thus, depending on the content, the image may now appear less sharp or even distorted.

Many consumer projectors will only have vertical correction, where the projector is placed on the center axis of the surface horizontally, but is too far above or below the center axis, likely to prevent the projector from being a viewer obstruction. Unfortunately, this will not help if the projector is off to the side. Usually, to add horizontal keystone correction will require a slightly more expensive projector to add the additional processing of the image. When these corrections are made, they are always equal. In other words, on a vertical correction, the same number of pixels left and right will be adjusted, which may not perfectly correct the image if the horizontal position is slightly off as well. By the time large venue projectors are used, keystone correction is often accomplished by adjusting each corner individually.

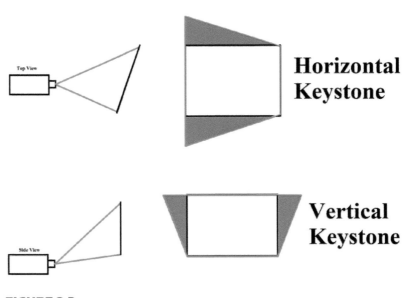

FIGURE 9.2
Keystone and its correction.

Adjusting for keystone may seem harmless, as it is an option in many projectors. However, this can create additional issues. When using a short throw lens—generally, any lens near a 1:1 ratio—the focal plane cannot always be met off axis. What this means is that even if the projector can digitally adjust to fit the image area, the image cannot be focused in its entirety. This means that if the projectionist works towards one end of the keystoned image, the opposite side will be out of focus. In order to minimize this, the projectionist should focus to the center of the image and allow the edges to be out of focus. This will generally only be noticeable with text, as it will be more difficult to read.

PIXEL ADJUSTMENT

Even when the image is free of keystone, the image may not fit perfectly on the surface. When this happens, most projectors will have the ability to adjust the incoming image with pixel adjustment. There are a variety of adjustments available.

If the projectionist is unable to get the image small enough with lensing, and the image is overshooting the surface, there are two methods to fit the image. The first is digital zoom. This is the same principle that is used on the computer monitor when looking at an image. If the desire is to get it to fit a smaller area, then the image will be zoomed out, using less of the information to create the image. This still may not fit the surface as desired. The other method which is used is blanking. Blanking displays video black along the sides of the image, trimming it to fit the surface. It will always eliminate complete rows or columns; thus, it needs to work in conjunction with keystone correction if a diagonal correction is necessary. As with all digital adjustment, this does not change the source file, nor does it change the optical image. This means that the extra light may need to be absorbed through dark fabric or it may be observed in dark enough conditions.

With analog signals, the pixel clock may not always be aligned. The EDID for digital signals should never cause this issue. In either case, it is possible that the entirety of the image is not displayed. When looking at the menu for the pixel adjustment, one will notice that there are multiple entries for horizontal and vertical adjustment. You will find pixel total, pixel active, and pixel start for each direction. Depending on how the projector processes the signal, when it is digitally shifting the image and it exceeds the data available, the projector may blank the signal, or it may continue with the last available information. That would mean that if there were a solid line at the edge of the image, it would get thicker as that information repeated. In addition, the data on the leading edge would gradually be eliminated as it exceeded the display area. The acceptability of these changes really depends on the content being displayed.

GAMMA

Gamma is a function of the brightness of an image in a non-linear encoding and decoding of the luminance values. Displays will have a function of producing an image with an intensity-to-response curve in regard to brightness. If this curve is not showing the image as expected, then gamma correction can be applied to match displays. This is especially critical in order for the video operator to trust that the reference monitor matches what the audience can see. Gamma correction is most often used in IMAG situations, as the camera sees differently than the human eye and must be adjusted. As this has to do with the end display, this is where it is most often corrected. Individual displays may vary, which would require gamma to be corrected on each of them for them to all match. Correcting at the source will not likely be beneficial to the overall result.

COLOR CORRECTION

When using a single display, it may not matter if specific colors are slightly off. With that being said, specific color arrangements are often desired by the director or producer. Back in Chapter 1, we mentioned that the human eye is sensitive to a specific color range. We have also mentioned that different displays are also capable of creating a range of colors, which is often narrower than the human perception. This means that we sometimes will need to adjust the display to show colors as close as possible to what is expected.

When using multiple displays, even when they are not overlapping, we will need to apply color correction if they are within the field of view. In other words, if one display is in front of the viewer while the other is behind, color correction may not be necessary, as the viewer will be unable to compare the two. When making the adjustments, it is important to know that you will be adjusting down, never increasing from the start point. For instance, if displaying a white image on two displays, and one appears slightly "warmer" than the other, the operator will need to remove some of the red and green from one display, as it will be impossible to add it to the other. Conversely, the operator could reduce the blue in the other display, but may have to make a greater correction.

BRIGHTNESS

In a general sense, brightness is a completely perceived attribute of the display. In and of itself, this is not a measured attribute of any display, though it will be present in almost all sales literature. This does not mean that it is unimportant or that there are no quantifiable means of understanding how bright an image should be. After all, the image needs to have a bright enough presentation to be seen. The designer needs to understand how brightness is measured in order to specify the appropriate display device.

Lumens and Nits

Because brightness is perceived, standards have been enacted to take the guesswork out of matching individual perceptions. The amount of light that is being produced is a physical reality, though it is difficult to quantify without the proper tools. When we measure the projected area, we use the measurement of lumens. On the other hand, when we look at a display such as a monitor, we use nits. Essentially, one is the basis of a reflected light source, while the other is measuring the output of the light source.

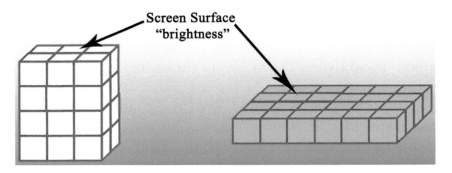

FIGURE 9.3
Brightness as compared to liquid volume.

A lumen is an international unit of luminous flux of light produced over a projected area. When light is projected from the device, it will be spread relatively evenly across a surface, though it will be brighter at the center. Consider a glass of water, which, when poured into a saucer, will have less depth while maintaining the same volume of space. The same happens with light. A narrower angle lens will concentrate the light, making it appear brighter than does a wide angle lens covering a greater surface area. The ANSI standard requires that manufacturers establish the projector in a controlled environment with less than 1% ambient light and an established contrast ratio, and with the projector in a presentation ready state. A white field is measured for lux/foot-candles at nine equidistant points, which are then averaged for the lumen value.

Lumens are an essential measurement for the presentation. The output of any given projector will likely not match that of the manufacturer, as there are many variables that come into play. These variables include the age of the projector, the age of the lamp (including the age of the reflector if the lamp housing is reused), and the power, especially since many projectors can run on variable power inputs. As most designers will not need to know these specifics, it is unlikely that measurements will be needed to taken on site, but the designer should be aware that there will likely be differences from manufacturer specifications. A general understanding of the formula is acceptable for most uses. To understand what the audience will see, the designer will need to determine the lumen output required.

When determining how bright the image should be, the designer needs to know how much ambient light is allowed to fall on the display surface, the desired contrast ratio (as determined by the content), and the area of the projection surface (which includes the blanked area of the image). We use a formula of lumens = $[(L * C) * A] / 0.75$, where L is the ambient light, C is the desired contrast ratio, and A is the area of the projection surface. If measuring the ambient light in lux, then make sure to measure the area in meters. The derating of 25% is due to the fact that there will be variables that will be difficult to measure, such as the age of the projector and the lamp, or not knowing the gain of the surface. There are no hard rules as to what contrast ratio needs to be achieved, but general rules will be discussed a bit later.

If the design is to use an emissive device for display, brightness is measured in nits. This is a metric unit where one foot-lambert equals 3.425 nits. As monitors and LED panels are the light source, larger displays do not diminish in brightness, due to the entire surface providing the light. As previously mentioned, emissive sources have much less concern with contrast ratio as compared to ambient light, but they do still need to be bright enough to see. In addition, the lumen formula for area is not necessary.

Stacking

When the formula for projection states that you should have a lumen output greater than what is available in a single projector, the design will call for stacking the image. This is a process of using multiple projectors with their images laid on top of one another to increase the overall brightness of the image. When using two equal projectors, the brightness is only doubled when presenting a white image. A frequent misunderstanding is that the lumen output will always be doubled. This is generally not the case, as it is often possible that the processing of the image will be timed slightly differently and not provide the doubled brightness. Thus, the brightness of a stacked image should also be de-rated. It should be noted that, just as video white is doubled, so is video black. This will have an effect on the contrast ratio of the displayed image.

While it is relatively simple to send the same signal to multiple projectors (such as when using a DA), this technique may add a considerable amount of time for alignment of the projectors, as well as for maintaining the image day to day. As can be seen in Figure 9.4, the stacked image can run into issues when used on a non-standard surface. The focal plane of the projector is designed for a projection screen. Additional considerations will need to be made for varying distances or off-axis projection. The term stacking applies to the image, not necessarily the position of the projectors. It is preferred for the projectors to be physically stacked one over another, as the alignment process is considerably easier because many large venue projectors

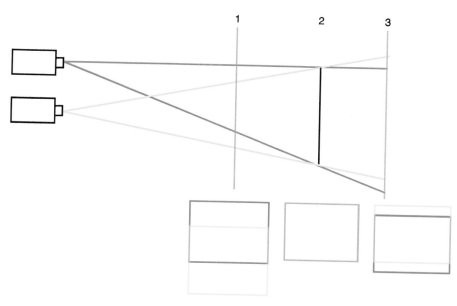

FIGURE 9.4
Stacking the image.

are equipped with stacking hardware. As those projectors are also equipped with lens shift, the alignment is simplified.

CONTRAST RATIO

As previously mentioned, the contrast ratio is the comparison of light to dark. In the specification of a projector, ANSI standards are very clear and are the best measurement to use for the presentation specifications. When manufacturers do not specify ANSI contrast ratio, then they are likely comparing full white and full black fields. Occasionally, there will be stated a dynamic contrast, which is generally inflated by reducing the overall lumen output to achieve this result. As was discussed in the section on display surfaces, two sources of light will greatly affect the overall contrast ratio, the ambient light in the room, and video black.

Video Black

Whenever a projector is not displaying a video signal, it still produces some amount of light. This light is known as video black. Every lamp based display (including monitors that are not using solid state lighting) will produce video black. This light comes from that which cannot be contained within the display, which includes monitors which use lamp technology for their illumination. DLP and LCOS displays tend to have better retention of the light, creating better black levels. As light is additive, each source of light added to the display (especially with stacked images) will raise the black level. This will change the overall contrast ratio of the image as the new, brighter black level is greater than the original black level of a single projector. This will need to be taken into account, as it may create the need for an even brighter display or a compromise for a single display.

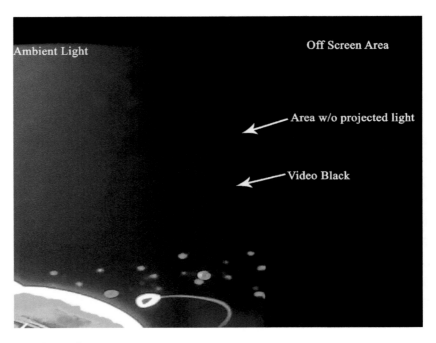

FIGURE 9.5
Evidence of video black on projection screen.

Ambient Light

While ambient light is not part of the manufacturers' specifications on contrast ratio, as the ANSI standards specify the allowed amount, it will be of great interest to the design of the show. It does not take a lot of ambient light to change the contrast ratio of the presented image. Again, the amount of contrast required depends on the content. As not all light sources are of the same color temperature, ambient light can change the way the projected image looks.

CHAPTER 10
Troubleshooting

Even with a lot of planning and preparation, mistakes can be made, either through execution or faulty equipment. In this section, we hope to help identify common issues which may occur that will prevent the perfect execution of the design. As with all parts of the system, knowing how each piece works will ultimately play into getting it all to work. If there is not an understanding of how it should work at each point, then it is impossible to diagnose the problem.

In addition, never be afraid to actually read the manuals for your equipment. Even if you purchased your equipment used, the internet is a wonderful resource for finding manuals. In addition, there are forums for specific media servers, as well as general theatrical forums with professionals who share information with one another to solve problems. There is a good chance that someone has run into a similar situation and you can work it out together. If you are working on something completely unfamiliar, make sure that your tech period gives you the time to experiment and solve challenges that arrive. Tech support may not be available late at night or on the weekends when you really need it.

GROUNDING AND SHIELDING

Noise due to improper grounding or shielding can be just as annoying in a video system as it is in an audio system. In audio, this noise is an audible buzz or hum. In a video system, it can present itself as "hum bars" or static. Before we get too deep into trying to fix the issue, we must understand what is going on and what are good and bad methods of trying to fix it. This type of interference is commonly known as a ground loop.

There are two types of grounding which building codes require. (I am speaking primarily of the United States, so always check local codes.) The first type of grounding is known as system grounding. This is the connection to the earth of a conductor which normally carries current, i.e. the neutral line or grounded

213

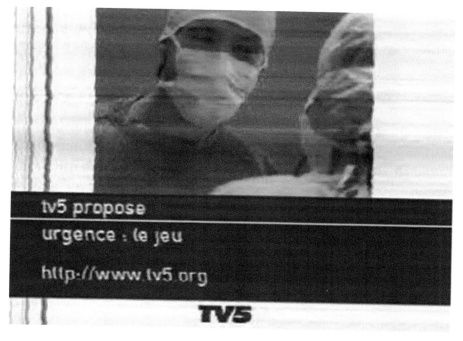

FIGURE 10.1

Hum bars in a video system.

Source: Ming J. Zhou

conductor. This is a safety system which is required to protect against lightning. The second is known as equipment grounding. This is ensuring that all exposed electrical equipment is bonded to ground. This prevents the possibility of the equipment becoming energized due to equipment faults.

Common mode and differential mode are two more important ideas to keep in mind in regard to bonding. The differential mode is what is used to carry the signal (or control voltage) on the cable in an analog system. This voltage is one that exists between the wires running together within a cable. At any given time, the currents between the two wires should be equal and opposite. On the other hand, the common mode voltage exists along the cable (fully end to end), and there is no voltage difference between the conductors. Common mode voltages in systems are almost always a form of noise. This comes from equipment being grounded at different points. In addition, the cables can act as receiving antennas for radio signals, which is known as noise coupling mechanisms.

There is a third type of grounding, which is where our troubleshooting comes to play. This is known as technical grounding. This is a scheme of bonding between the equipment grounding of the technical equipment in order to prevent noise in the system. The noise to be eliminated is a result of power-related noise currents on the shields of the signal wiring. Technical grounding still needs to provide equipment grounding required for safety, so this can become challenging. It should also keep shielding required to protect against radio frequency interference.

Noise within the system can have a number of causes. Improper shield termination within the equipment, cable imbalance (which lets in common mode noise), capacitance imbalance of the cable, and inadequate shielding of internal wiring, as well as shield current induced noise (which is an inductive imbalance between the shield and signal conductors) are all factors which may create noise within the system.

However, noise can also get into the system even when there are no wires in common between components of the system. This noise comes by means of some type of field, the first of which is a magnetic field which surrounds the wire carrying the signal. It is also possible that interference comes from an electric field, which is the voltage difference between two charged conductors. Then there is the electromagnetic field, which comes in the form of radio waves and is a combination of magnetic and electric fields at right angles to one another.

The move to digital transmission of video signals has made this less of an issue overall. For analog signals, there are good and bad ways to eliminate the noise from a system. First of all, a common method that should never be employed is the defeating of the equipment ground (Figure 10.2). There have been a number of times that it has been observed that power cables have had the grounding pin removed or grounding adapters have been used. Grounding adapters are often misused; they are meant to redirect the ground, not remove it. A grounding adapter could be used in a testing situation when looking to find the source of interference but should never be used in a production environment. The removal of the ground increases the risk of electric shock.

A video ground loop isolator, sometimes known as a humbucker, is often the fastest and best option for eliminating noise in the system. The isolator eliminates the connection between the grounding connections of two pieces of equipment through the use of a transformer. As the noise is created by different parts of the system having different ground potentials, this is the best solution when it is not possible to have

FIGURE 10.2
Ground lift adapter should only be used for testing, and you should never remove the ground pin.

isolated power with a common ground. As the display is often the part of the system that is on a different ground, placing the hum-bucker just before the display will probably be the best method to reduce the noise. That being said, if you have the time to track down the problem, it is best to do so. When you do, start at the display and work your way backwards.

216

FIGURE 10.3
A hum-bucker is a great way to defeat a ground loop.

When tracing a grounding issue in a co-axial cable (including multiple co-axial cables in component or RGBHV), it is possible to use a clamp-on ammeter. This is a "leakage" tester that can measure low currents at 1 mA or better, and it can easily finding a conductor carrying current. As a signal current in a co-axial cable should generate equal but opposing fields, they should be cancelled out and not show a "leak". With a ground loop, since its current does not return on the same cable, the meter can determine the ground loop. This likely prevents the need to disconnect everything.

As electromagnetic interference will affect digital signals as well as analog ones, there are additional means that may be considered that will work with both systems. RF interference can be minimized either through ferrite cores which can be installed over cables or by purchasing cables with cores as part of the cable build. The add-on variety is a core that connects around the cable. When possible, pass the cable through more than once (creating a loop around the clamshell) to increase the effectiveness. This should be added near the end of the cable. This can be particularly helpful because we often coil our cable to neaten the clutter, but this makes a much better antenna when we do so.

Choosing a fiber optic run between the source and the display can often offer a worry-free installation. Noise in the system is completely divided and should be an easy fix. The other relatively easy fix is in cable management. Bundling video lines in a snake can sometimes cancel out stray magnetic fields. Make sure that when crossing power lines, especially power that is attached to dimmers, the path is perpendicular. When video lines run along or near lighting cables, there is a very good chance that noise will be added to the video system. This can be difficult when both the lighting and the projection are flown on the same truss. If this is the case, first try to isolate

FIGURE 10.4
An HDMI cable built with a ferrite core.

the projector from the truss (work with the riggers in using truss protectors if possible). Also, if the data lines and power lines must run from the same side of the stage, have separate cable picks and run the cables on opposite sides of the truss. Planning ahead will save a lot of headaches later.

SKEW

Skew is a video distortion caused by the late arrival of one or more colored systems due to sending signals over twisted pair cables. The delayed color signals will be shifted to the right of the faster "on-time" colors. This will look bad and can cause eye fatigue for the audience (when minimal skewing is present). The twisting of data grade Ethernet cables at different rates is intended to reduce cross talk between the pairs. Thus, the longer the cable, the greater the time it takes for some pairs to deliver information than others. The greater the resolution and refresh rate (total bandwidth) of a signal, the greater the variance in timing. Skew can happen in as little as three feet.

In order to eliminate skew, the designer can utilize skew-free cables, such as those manufactured by Extron. These cables look like standard UTP cables, but they have equal twist patterns for all of the twisted pair. It is also possible to add skew compensation cables at the end of a run. These are basically co-axial patch cables of various lengths that are added in order to compensate. In order to know how much you would need to add, you would need to use a twisted pair cable tester to find out the length of the run, and then add the corresponding difference. This is not ideal since the purpose of using video baluns is to be able to use inexpensive category cable and be done with it.

If the video balun does not have a skew correction, then the other option is to use a skew equalizer. This is a separate piece of equipment with a rotary dial that will delay the faster lines. Obviously, when all is said and done, you may have to work with audio to re-synchronize the video and audio. After all, just a few milliseconds can be noticeable.

219

SIGNAL STRENGTH

Video signals, similar to audio signals, are measured in decibels in regard to their signal strength. The more times that the signal is split and not refreshed, the more that signal will degrade. The same will happen with extremely long runs of distribution cables. Each type of signal and cable has its own standard. As the signal gets weaker, more issues arrive in the video display. Signals with higher resolution and refresh rates will take up more bandwidth and will suffer more with any signal degradation.

In an analog system, most of us are aware of "snow" in the image of a weak TV signal. In a digital system, the signal will result in choppy, highly digitized artifacts or will not display at all. Not all sources start out with the same signal strength.

An integrated graphics card will likely have less power than a discrete graphics card. Using digital amplifiers to boost the strength of a run, as well as re-clocking the signal, is good practice for long runs. Any cable that comes near the recommended length of a signal on a cable should be considered long.

SYNC

A video signal which is not synchronized is a problem. This can go beyond the scope of the timing of colors in a skewed cable. This is more than an issue with audio and video timing being off. Video synchronization can make or break a signal entirely. When you are using a cable which has all of its wiring combined, there are a few issues that can arise. However, with an RGBHV signal, using a 5-wire co-axial bundle, it can be easy to switch the two sync cables, as there is no uniform color code for those wires. If they are switched, then there will be no signal displayed. In addition, if one of them is damaged, it is possible that there will be no signal. A general rule of thumb when connecting the sync cables is to use the lighter color as the horizontal sync.

Genlock

Not all synchronization problems are so easily solved. For a single projector or single monitor, the audience will not notice any synchronization issues other than what might occur with audio (a separate type of issue). With a still image, they will also be unlikely to notice. However, when we add multiple displays, or displays with multiple components, such as a video wall, then it may become a problem. Each display will refresh its content based on the signal as it arrives. This can appear as a staggered refresh, which could be distracting at most, or, in the case of a video wall, there could be a tearing of the image. As was seen in Figure 4.10, where the LED wall was taller than a 1080 display (thus requiring a secondary media server for the upper portion), it is possible that motion between the two servers may not match exactly, making it appear as if the display were torn at the division and one portion displays the image at a slightly different timing.

With all of these variables, it could be very frustrating to use more than one display. Once again, we borrow from the broadcast industry, which has tackled this back to the beginning of video. We need to get the displays to refresh starting at the same time as the sources feeding them. To do this, we need a reference—something that will be common to the system. This is a bit of equipment known as a black burst generator.

In an analog system, this is a bi-level frequency generator. In an HD system, the bi-level generator will still work, but a tri-level sync pulse will work better (to sync the chrominance). The generator itself will not solve the issues alone. Beyond that, there needs to be a commonality among the system, achieved through generator locking (genlock), which allows all of the connected system to use the common reference, giving identical horizontal and vertical timing. This does not pass through the same lines as the rest of the video signal, but is a separate co-axial distribution. The genlock is not for the displays themselves, but for the control and distribution portion of the system. On many switchers and other distribution equipment, there will be a genlock input and thru port built in. Sources such as media servers may also have genlock capabilities so they can all be connected.

If there is a sync issue and a device does not have genlock capabilities, there is one additional device that can be added. This is a time based corrector (TBC), also called a frame synchronizer. For most live performance, the addition of this device may not be ideal. With modern equipment it is less likely to be used. In order for the devices to be synced, the TBC must delay some signals in order to have all of them begin together.

While it is unlikely, this could add latency up to two frames. A frame synchronizer will actually buffer full frames in order to accomplish the same principle. If a system must be created using a passive switcher, utilizing a frame synchronizer will minimize problems—if not completely eliminating them—during the switching process, providing a better transition for the audience.

EDID/Handshake

In the process of connecting multiple devices together, there is the risk of communication error that will interfere with the proper display of the image. Though this is not entirely a synchronization of the image, there needs to be a common communication of data transfer, which needs to agree in order to display the image. Extended Display Identification Data (EDID) allows a graphics card to synchronize with the display. However, this data was intended to be communicated directly between the two devices. As we build bigger, more complex video systems, the transfer of this data will occur through several devices between the source and the display, interrupting this transmission.

There are a few challenges that can occur, especially when the designer will need to use more legacy devices. In modern equipment, when a device is powered off, there are usually some parts of the system that are still running. One such part will be a serial programmable read-only memory (PROM), or an electrically erasable PROM (EEPROM), which stores the EDID. This memory prevents the need to power on the devices in a particular order. Instead, the source can have the ability to read the EDID and establish a handshake with the display before the display is powered on and ready to display an image. Legacy devices may not have this available, which will require having to power on the system and having it fully operational from the display back to the source.

In addition to the transfer of EDID, there is the process of "handshaking", which is a process that allows negotiation between the source and additional devices to the display. This establishes a set of rules for how the devices will communicate. In some ways, this is beneficial, as it can allow communication as to whether or not data is being successfully transmitted. It can also be used as a portion of HDCP, which can cause issues, especially if there are devices using different versions.

Depending on the device, especially with computer graphics cards, EDID and the handshake may or may not be "hot swappable". In other words, if a device is disconnected and another device is connected, the transmission of the rules of connection may or may not happen. If the rules are not transmitted, the image will not be displayed. If this is the case, the only option is restarting the source after the new connections have been made. In addition, when multiple devices are present between the source and display (such as switchers, fiber optic distribution, and DAs), then there may not be the ability for the source to get the information. If this is the case, the best-case scenario will be to employ an EDID emulator immediately after the source. Some switchers can be programmed to send out a generated EDID.

DIGITAL ARTIFACTS

A digital artifact is not something that modern archaeologists are hunting for, or at least not for the purposes of this text. Instead, this is an unintended error in the data for the digital image. There are many causes for these errors and it may take a bit of investigation to track down and eliminate these errors.

Sources for digital artifacts can come from the source itself, especially if it is a computer. Errors can be generated from overheating within the computer, either due to overclocking the CPU or GPU, or due to poor thermal management. This can cause pixelization of the video or stuttering as it ramps back output to minimize heat generation.

Artifacts can also arise in the distribution. As was mentioned, lack of signal strength can result in lost data to the display. When this happens, there may be no display at all, a stuttering image, or, at best, pixelization, with the majority of the image being presented. Boosting the signal strength or reducing the bandwidth requirements can often help here, but there also could just be poor connections or damage to the cables. Cables are designed with the intent of being installed and the connections being broken infrequently. In entertainment, the connections are broken frequently, gradually causing wear or other damage to the connectors. Terminations which rely on compression (such as HDMI) may wear down and no longer make good connections. The bad connection is often intermittent, as bumping cables can cause the signal to come and go. For equipment that is regularly connected and disconnected, having an external patch bay will save on repairing connections on the equipment.

Besides the hardware, there could be errors in the software in the decoding of the video stream. This may be less likely than an error that originates with the source file and is not seen until the image is shown on a larger scale. If the error originated with the compression or other steps in creation of the content, then there will be little that can be done after the fact. For instance, a rolling shutter can create an artifact that is due to a fast-moving object that the image sensor captures incorrectly, such as a vertical line appearing to be slanted. Lossy compression techniques may yield artifacts which will be present during playback. Another type of artifact is often described as "noise". This can be the result of poor color range (low bit depth), low resolution being displayed at a much higher resolution, and halos (contrast boundary error) as a result of exposure. Sometimes this can be fixed by rendering the content again (checking the settings on your NLE), while others may require building the content again.

Another type of digital artifact that will come from the creation process is called moiré. This is an artificial banding or rippling in the image. This can come from the spatial frequencies of the object being recorded (for example, a fabric pattern or banding on a rolltop desk). This can occur in a lower quality camera that has a poor anti-aliasing filter and is quite common when using a Digital Single-Lens Reflex camera (DSLR) for recording. Many consumers have found that a digital camera can be a wonderful tool for recording video as well. Unfortunately, the video recording is at a much lower resolution, because the

FIGURE 10.5
Moiré effect in a video, resulting from photographing the display.

camera is designed for photography. To achieve the recording, the DSLR skips parts of its resolution, as opposed to recording the full resolution, and utilizes a quality down-conversion algorithm. A quality video camera uses an optical low pass filter which smooths fine details that may cause artifacts during playback.

DROPPED FRAMES

On occasion we will display the video and all looks fine except that every once in a while the screen will go blank for a split second and then continue to play as normal. This is not a sync issue as described above, but it is simply a dropped frame. As with most challenges, there are a few things that can cause this. First, determine whether the frames are dropped (missing) from the original source file. If the original file is good, then there are a few things to consider in the playback system.

With many small production companies, there is often the challenge to multi-task as much as possible, which often includes the video computer. If the computer is not sufficiently designed, having it try and run multiple tasks during a production can cause some frames of video to not be produced, as the computer is trying to keep up. Many media programs will put the processing of the video onto the GPU to improve rendering, and this should hopefully prevent this. If the computer does not have a discrete graphics card, then this cannot happen. In addition, during a production, make sure that the computer is only running software that is critical to the production (no background software, especially anti-virus software). It should be stressed that dedicated computers are the best solution; they should not be connected to the internet, if possible. The CPU and GPU usage can be monitored to see if you are overtaxing the system. If everything has been checked, ensuring that unnecessary background applications are off, only necessary programs are running, and the system is properly configured for those programs, but the processors are being maxed, then changing to a less demanding codec may be necessary. In addition, if your playback is rendering a preview at the same time as program (the output to the audience display), minimizing how much is dedicated to the preview (not full screen) may yield more processing power for the program image.

As with all electronics, heat will cause issues. It is better that the ambient temperature in the equipment space is relatively cool (the operator might need long sleeves) so that air-cooled devices have a better chance to dissipate heat. Even when a processor is not overclocked (told to process at greater than recommended speeds), if the ambient temperature is too high, or airflow is restricted due to placement of the equipment, or if the equipment has not been maintained and is too dusty inside, then the processors can have problems. Some will slow themselves down, appearing to have a jittery moving image, while others may drop frames, while others may try to keep up and end up having physical failures. In addition, the HDD may end up not reading correctly, providing missed data to process. A good practice should be to give the system a rest, possibly shutting down every night, even though normal operation should allow the computer to run continuously. This will also help to close background operations that may still be running that the user was not aware were using precious resources.

227

If the computer is offline, as recommended, then a part of a maintenance plan should be to keep drivers up to date. Obviously, if the newest driver does not solve the problem, or worsens it, then you can always roll back to the previous known good driver. If your computer is built by a major company, it may be easy to find all applicable driver updates, as you should be able to download them from their website. If you have built your own computer or modified it in any way, then you will have to do more of your own legwork. Also, make sure to keep up to date on your media server software, as there may be bug fixes in their updates.

Another part of the maintenance plan should be storage management. Hopefully, as suggested, the production is using a dedicated computer. If you are using an HDD, then it should be properly maintained by removing unnecessary files and making sure that you do not have fragmented files. The less that the drive needs to search for bits of the files, then the less chance there is that a frame will arrive without the full data and be dropped.

Finally, check once again that your playback system and content are compatible and that all options are optimally set. Ideally, all of the content will be matched so that playback options will be set for one type of video. This means that all codecs are the same, with the same color space, the same frame rate, and any other options available. If the media player is set to display at a lower frame rate than the content, there is the potential for a less smooth image in fast-moving video, but at least there is the greater probability that there will not be a dropped frame.

LATENCY

Entertainment is based on timeliness. Cues are called and results are expected to happen. The video operator may take the cue on time, but there is a delay in the timing of the displayed image. This is not the fault of one component, but a symptom of a problem in the overall system. Latency is a slowing in the time it takes to display content due to processing speeds of various components in the system. This is most prevalent when live video is being displayed, as playback does not have the same impact on the production.

When there is latency in an IMAG system, audio and video may not properly synchronize, and the result looks like a poorly dubbed movie. While the audio can be delayed to match the video, the audience may still notice that there is a delay between the performer and the observed image. In addition, latency can be problematic in a CCTV where a conductor/singer/musician relies on accuracy for timing. In that same system, the stage manager may rely on timing accuracy for calling cues, or automation operators may rely on it for safe movement of scenery. While some theaters may continue to rely on analog systems that do not have latency issues (for CCTV applications), the low resolution and lesser video quality preclude them for use in IMAG and they will become more difficult to maintain in the long run.

The designer and the design team should be choosing components of the system with latency in mind. Something that is advertised as "no latency" should be processing video at less than 100 ms. Something advertised as "low latency" may still have some, but it will be very low, preferably below 10 ms. There is no absolute value for either of these terms. Each component in the system will require some amount of processing time, even if it is only a few milliseconds. Remember that if we use the NTSC standard of 29.97 fps, then each frame takes approximately 33.4 ms to be shown. This means that something that is "low latency" can by itself delay an image by almost three frames, which may or may not be perceptible to the audience. With multiple devices, it is easy to see how an image can be delayed and this can become noticeable.

The biggest contributors to latency are any devices that require temporal storage (buffering). Devices such as DAs are low contributors to the latency issue, as they are not processing the signal in this fashion. The amount of data that has to be stored before the data can be passed down the distribution chain can be a few pixels to a few frames. Since the decoding of the file is using a variable bit rate (depending on how it is compressed), then this storage allows for uninterrupted display.

Processing of the video signal and the resultant latency can also be an issue when the media design included interactivity. If there is too great of a delay in response between the interactive device and the resultant display, the effect to be achieved can be ruined. For this reason, the system design may end up becoming more complicated than originally conceived, as portions requiring low latency may end up being routed separately from other portions only requiring playback. For this reason, even though media servers can easily handle a live video input, they may add too much latency, so that the designer will instead put a switching device after the media server and have the cameras go through that as well, since it adds less latency to the live video stream.

CONTENT PLAYBACK ERRORS

As we continue through the system, looking for potential errors, the content itself may be at issue. We have looked at several factors in unintended issues. Here are a few more things to consider when the content does not play as expected. These are with regard to digital systems, not including optical disk playback systems such as DVD.

Almost any playback issue that is directly related to the content likely has correlation to the codec. In addition to a codec being not optimal for any given computer system —such as requiring too much processing power to properly display the content, as previously discussed—the content might not play at all. The computer, first of all, needs to have the proper codec installed to be able to process the video. If it cannot decode the video, then it cannot play the video. In addition, the playback system to be used will need to be able to utilize that codec (older playback systems may not be able to use modern codecs). Many media servers will designate what kind of codecs can be input, and they still will convert the content to a unified codec from there. Some programs do not play the content directly, but merely reference the video files (and manipulate them) and are optimized by using the native playback of the OS.

DISPLAY ERRORS

It is possible that the operator is able to play the content, and checks that it is showing on the reference monitor, but still the display is not what is expected. Even if the video system is relatively simple, such as a single player being distributed to multiple displays through a DA, the image may not play back to fill the display area. This is likely not a problem with the content, but in the system of how the EDID is managed. As the DA takes the EDID from the local monitor, which is likely where the operator has connected the reference monitor, this may not match the display EDID. For instance, if the display is full HD (1920x1080), but the monitor is not at full HD, say 1600x900, then the displayed image will be smaller than the full display. To rectify this, the local monitor EDID needs to match the display (EDID emulator or different monitor), or the display will require digital adjustment or zoom to fit (not a bad option when rear projecting). The former is preferable, as the content was likely designed for the display, and the latter solutions will degrade the image. Conversely, in a 4:3 aspect ratio, a common large venue projector resolution is 1400x1050, but there were no native monitors made at that resolution. They were made at 1600x1200, at the closest resolution. This leaves the design team with fewer corrective options.

Another common display error is when the wrong color space is displayed. The display and the content, as well as any part of the distribution system that can control the color space, must be consistent. If there is a drastic difference in color between what is seen on screen and what is intended to be displayed then this is one of the likely culprits. In Figure 10.6, the same monitor is shown with color bars being sent with the wrong color space and the correct color space. It is possible that a

231

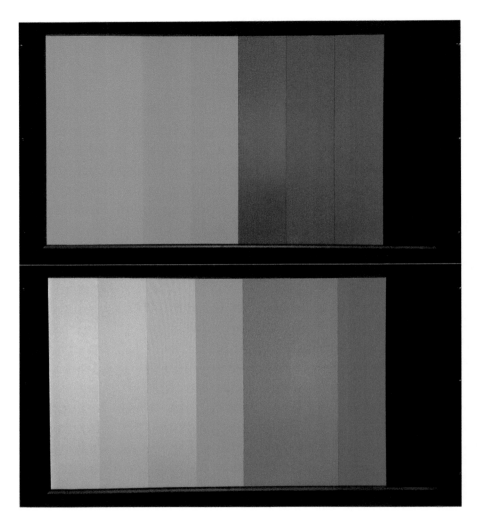

FIGURE 10.6
YPbPr color space as displayed on an RGB system compared to correctly displayed color bars.

similar incorrect look would appear if part of the distribution cables were damaged or incorrectly connected.

CONTROL ERRORS

When it is time to take the cue to play the content, the operator expects that executing the cue will make it happen. What are possible reasons that there could be a control error? There are many issues which may arise that cannot be discussed here, as they would be symptoms of a particular piece of gear, but we will look at a common issue which is more generic.

Assuming that all control cables have been checked, including the proper orientation of MIDI in/out connections, that USB controllers are fully seated, and that any other physical connection does not suffer from an air gap, then we can look at some other common problems. Something that has been witnessed a number of times is that when a computer program is being used for playback, it can be deselected as the active program. Certainly, it will still be running in the background, but if the operator selects another function of the computer (maybe checking on a file), then the playback program may no longer accept user input until it is properly selected as active.

NETWORK ERRORS

As the network is the extra glue which allows ease of use to the operator, for a multitude of reasons, it can be extremely frustrating when it does not work. The most common error is addressing. Make sure to double-check the address on the equipment that is not responding. Sometimes two pieces of equipment will have inadvertently been addressed the same, which will cause both of them to not respond. All of the addresses need to be valid for that range. Make sure that the subnet matches your network.

233

If the addressing and all other settings are correct, there is possibly a problem in the physical equipment. Make sure that any switches and routers are properly configured and functioning. A bad power supply can be frustrating. Ethernet cables can be fragile. A good cable tester can tell how far along the line a break is detected. The RJ-45 connectors can also be damaged. If the locking tab fails to keep a secure connection, data can fail to transmit. At the connection, there should be two small LED indicators which can identify whether there is a connection and data transfer. If using wireless transmission through a bridge or router, then you may need to see how noisy the band and channel for your space might be. Some simple changes here can speed up transmission and reduce lost packets.

PREVENTIVE MAINTENANCE

As with an automobile, projectors and other video equipment need regular checkups and tune-ups to remain functioning and dependably. The maintenance required on your equipment will vary depending on the type, how often it is used, and the environment in which it is used. By understanding why maintenance is necessary and learning the basic techniques, you should be able to begin making a proper maintenance program and avoid common failures.

Preventive maintenance is always about reliability: averting disaster in the middle of a production. While this could be misconstrued as being told that you purchased faulty equipment that cannot run without intervention, this is far from the case. The second biggest reason to properly maintain your equipment is purely financial. This can help avert costly repairs or even premature total failure. Going back to the vehicle metaphor, whether you drive a top-of-the-line car or the inexpensive import, both will end up failing if not properly maintained. While many drivers receive education about vehicle maintenance when taking a driver's education course, the same does not apply to other technology. The manufacturers will offer it, but the owner of the equipment does not always provide the means to get that education.

There are many factors that lead to failure in video equipment. First and foremost, you need to consider the environment in which you have equipment such as a projector. In a nightclub or even many theater applications, a projector is constantly subject to dust and fog or haze particles. There will be plenty of discussion about how this affects the various components of a projector, but first, consider heat. Most projectors have some type of filtration device to limit the amount of particulates entering the projector housing. If you have your projector in a dusty environment, you may find either that the filter is not dense enough and causes too many particles to get inside your projector or that the filter is adequate and needs to be cleaned or replaced frequently. You will probably find this out within the first few months of operation. If the particles are allowed to get inside of the projector, you will end up with a wide variety of problems, including coating heat sinks, potentially causing components to overheat. If you have an adequate filter but do not clean or change the filter often enough, you will limit the amount of air flow and the ability for the components to cool, which can result in component failure and shorter lamp life.

Now, to continue with the hazards of heat, there are other factors to consider. When turning off a projector after use, it is necessary to use the proper procedure listed in your user manual. The reason this is crucial is that there will be an abundance of heat built up inside the projector even if it is used for only five minutes. All components will have a greater chance of failure if not cooled properly; plus, lamps are more prone to damage if moved prior to being fully cooled. Generally, when a projector is shut down in the proper manner, the lamp will be de-arced and the cooling fans will run at a higher speed for a few minutes. When the fans have stopped, the projector should be cool enough to remove power. If power is cut and the fans are unable to continue to cool the projector properly, the heat from the lamp will actually show a rise in temperature in the surrounding components initially, before naturally cooling.

You need to monitor the use of your projector to ensure that you are not causing stress on the components. The most common failure by users is neglecting to monitor the hours used on a lamp, or intentionally overusing the lamp due to the cost of a replacement. The manufacturer will provide you with the amount of hours a lamp should be used. Unlike when you use a lamp in a lighting fixture, you do not want to push a projector lamp until it fails. After a lamp reaches a certain point in its life cycle, it may start emitting a higher degree of infrared light, which can damage the light engine, resulting in poor color or possible failure. Another potential problem is that running a lamp to the point of failure may produce an explosion, sending fragments into other parts of the projector. Although projector lamps are expensive, and there is the temptation for using them until failure, you can easily negate your savings by neglectfully causing other internal damage, and potential health hazards if the lamp contains mercury. On some professional projectors, you may have the option of connecting to the projector with an internet browser, allowing for greater monitoring of internal temperatures and other potential failures, potentially even having the projector email alerts.

Besides dust clogging air filters or accumulating on heat sinks, it can cause havoc with your optics. At this point, it is recommended to not clean the optics with anything other than air (low psi compressed air or a lens blower). If your lens has an accumulation of contaminants, such as oils from atmospherics or fingerprints, you may need to clean the lens. The manual should include a recommended practice for your particular model, but an important thing to consider is that the lens can scratch fairly easily and that it will have a coating that most cleaners will destroy. The lens is a particularly expensive component to your projector and is not something that you want to replace, so be careful. Dust can also cause problems with your internal optics as well. LCD projectors are particularly at risk for dust, as the optics train is usually not a sealed component. When the dust settles on the panels, it traps heat, which will cause premature failure or discoloration of your image. You will start to notice the increase of contaminants in your optics when you take your image out of focus.

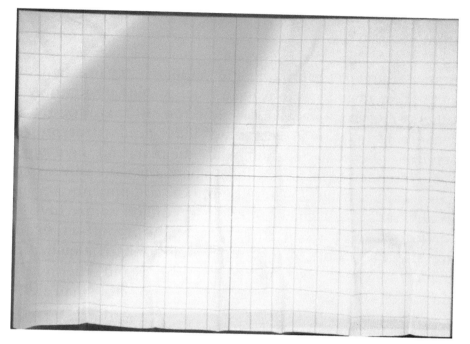

FIGURE 10.7
Delamination of 3-chip DLP prism.

The question often arises as to who should provide the maintenance. First of all, consult your user manual for recommendations about timing for different maintenance options. It will clearly explain the extent of the user's ability to perform certain maintenance and what must be done by a qualified technician, especially in order to maintain a warranty. Most repair facilities will give you the option of sending in a projector for cleaning, or will send a technician to your property if you have multiple projectors. In the end, a regular maintenance routine may cost a couple of hundred dollars per year, but an improperly maintained projector can easily cost 75% of the initial purchase price in a short amount of time. Sometimes, failures happen that can take an otherwise functioning piece of gear and turn it into spare parts. Such is the case above, where the failure in the prism makes the image unusable. Preventive maintenance may or may not have been able to prevent this from occurring.

Some failures are inevitable and ultimately repairable. One of the best advantages to using a rental staging projector over other professional installation projectors is the ease of maintenance. Installation projectors will likely need to be sent to a service facility to be repaired, while the rental staging projector is intended to be greatly field serviceable. One failure that can ruin the image is when the optical components are out of alignment (convergence). End users can be trained to field service this, but make sure that you have the proper training, as any attempt to work on a powered projector has extreme risks that could lead to severe injury or death.

238

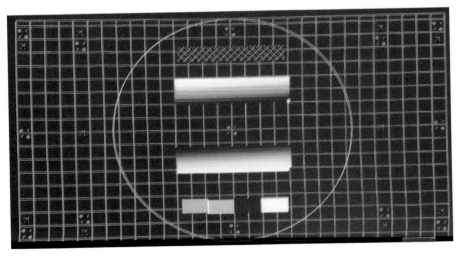

FIGURE 10.8
Projector out of convergence.

CHAPTER 11

Advanced Projection Design

After you have mastered basic media design, there will be a desire to take it to the next level. However, if the basics are not mastered, this can be a frustrating next step. Advanced projection techniques used in spectacular productions are seen all over the internet. These productions use multiple displays of varying types, with massive processing and distribution. In this section, we will introduce what is needed to accomplish these grand and magical designs.

VIDEO MAPPING AND MASKING

When going beyond the basic backdrop, the designer will need to take additional measures. There are two principles at work, which can work individually or in tandem, depending on the surface. This is where projection truly has the opportunity to stand out.

Masking Irregular Shaped Objects

The shape of a projected image is determined by the image processor and the geometry of the projection. In other words, it is a rectangular image which may be altered due to being off axis. If the set design does not match that shape, then we mask the projection. A mask is used to hide that which we do not want to see, and it makes the set seem more like it has been painted with the light. In the realm of projection, this means projecting black over portions of the image. This is different than keystone correction, which blanks a portion of the projected image, because this does not transform the image at all.

There are a number of ways to do this, some easier than others. The simplest method, especially for those who are new to advanced projection, will be to wait until the system is completely installed before beginning. At this point, the designer will create a mask to be inserted into the media server. This is accomplished by using a drawing program and projecting a full raster of white. Then, "paint" black on all areas that should not be seen. When this file is put into the media server as a masking layer, the white areas of the image are where the image will appear, while the black will remain as video black. This works with static sets. So, as long as there is no change in scenery, or there is accurate placement when the sets change, this method will work perfectly. The designer can make as many masks as needed, adding each one appropriately, depending on the scene.

This method may be too time-consuming for setup prior to the performance. At this point, the designer will rely on pre-visualizations. The set designer can provide a rendering of what the set should look like. The media designer should be able to understand the position of the projectors and the type of image that they will be creating. A computer aided design (CAD) or "what you see is what you get" (WYSIWYG) type of program will aid in this. The designer can create a mask before arriving on site and then alter it as needed for fine detailing. This mask can even be applied when creating the content (applied in the non-linear editor, or NLE), which can save on processing power. This allows for less adjustment on site. If access to computer aided tools is unavailable, the designer may be able to use a photograph, as long as it is taken from the point of where the projector will be positioned and the set will not move. The use of a focus grid in the photograph will aid in accurately lining up the image.

FIGURE 11.1
Masking an image to an irregular surface.

Source: Ian Shelanskey

In addition to the ability to take out the unwanted edges, masking can allow the designer to use one projector for multiple surfaces. As a media system can add considerable cost to a production, using less equipment can be beneficial. If the designer was looking for multiple screens but could only afford a single projector, then the raster could be sized to include all of the surfaces, blanking everything besides the screens. Obviously, this greatly reduces the resolution available for each surface, so this needs to be taken into account when creating the content. If the projection surfaces are not all on the same plane, there might be a need to play with selective focus, where some or all of the surfaces will have a soft focus. In addition, this puts video black over that entire area, which may need to be handled if the lighting designer requires a blackout.

Mapping 3D Objects

The next step after masking projection areas is to map them. This is the expanded portion of the other half of keystone correction, where the content is shaped to fit the surface. Projection mapping turns ordinary surfaces into a dynamic display. This allows for images to fill a three-dimensional space, breaking from the confines of the traditional two dimensions. While it is possible to accomplish this without specialized software, it is unlikely that a designer would attempt it unless absolutely necessary. Some large venue projectors will also have some very precise mapping software built in; sometimes this requires a separate purchase. As every software will handle this slightly different, this will be much more generalized than necessary to actually accomplish this out the door. Another thing to consider is that the warping process will add latency to the display, so remember to take this into account as well.

The projected image can be mapped to almost any shape that the light is able to reach. Complex surfaces, especially those where the audience will occupy a wide viewing angle, will require multiple projectors in multiple locations. This will increase the distribution network much more than when keeping the projectors together for more traditional presentations. If possible, project a focus grid, similar to when masking, and photograph it for beginning the mapping process.

It is a good idea to begin work in a virtual 3D modeling program. These programs are best used by those who use them

FIGURE 11.2
A single projector mapped on a model.

on a regular basis, which likely means that the designer will employ someone to help with this process. Inside the virtual space is where the bulk of the work on the files will be done. Video files are placed onto the virtual model as a texture. The designer will use a camera object in the program to represent the exact position of the projector. When the video is rendered at this point, it will be exactly as it needs to be in the "real" world. To increase accuracy, high budget productions have created the 3D model using Lidar (Light Detection and Ranging), which uses a pulsed laser to get accurate measurements.

In order to cover the intended area with projected light, it will require overshooting the area and masking the unwanted areas. This is all part of the mapping process and will not actually require a separate layer of masking, just as the keystone correction is all one process. It is just important to remember that you cannot stretch the projection in an area; you can only take away. As seen in Figure 11.2, mapping with a single projector may leave some areas without a projected image.

When you are creating a large image, which requires multiple projectors, there will also be a requirement for edge blending. We will discuss the ins and outs of this in just a bit. The first thing to remember is that the projector is designed to create an image on a flat plane perpendicular to the projector. This is where the best image is created. When we place our projectors, we want to be looking to create that scenario as close as possible for every projector to create the best-looking image and to cover the greatest amount of the surface. This means that when looking left to right, they may not all be projecting the next section of content, but instead are staggered, as the projected portions may be cross shooting one another. For instance, if the center portion of the set is set back from the sides, then two projectors may be necessary for the center—these are shooting to opposite sides of the stage, while the outer two are shooting directly towards the set (numbered 1,3,2,4 instead of 1,2,3,4).

In this case, the designer needs some different ideas of how to plan content. The two off-stage projectors will receive content that may have little need of mapping, unless they are required to also go into the center for part of the blend. The center two will have definite mapping for the environment that they are being presented in. This will require additional communication to the various parts of the team.

BLENDING

With an LED display, if the raster needs to be increased, then additional panels can be added, making the image to whatever size is required. With a projected image, there is the option of overshooting the display surface and masking the unwanted area, resulting in a loss of brightness (larger image) and a reduced number of pixels to create the image. The other option is to use multiple projectors to create a larger image.

The first instinct that a novice designer will have is to bring the images of two separate parts of the main image as close together as possible, aligning their edges. This is a process known as butting. The issue with butting the images together is that the likelihood of keeping a perfectly aligned edge without a noticeable seam (like a mullion in a video wall) is not very high. The other possibility is that the two images will slightly overlap, causing some blurring (pixels of different content overlapping) and a brighter portion of the image where they do overlap (physical property of combining light).

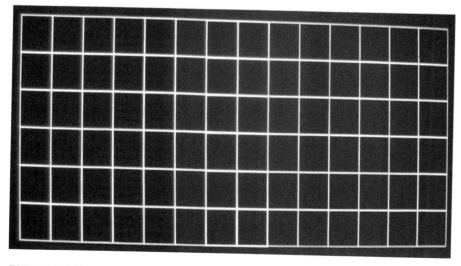

FIGURE 11.3
Aligning projectors for blending.

Instead of butting the images, the better way is to blend the image. In order to do this, we will have a smaller image than what would result with butted images. The reason for this is that we need to repeat some of the pixels from one image to another. As seen in Figure 11.3, the two projectors have the grid overlapped (fairly large blend zone for demonstration purposes). As was mentioned with butted images, the part of the image that overlaps is brighter, both in the grid as well as the video black (more on this later). Without the blending application, this would be unacceptable, but with the blending application, there will be a seamless image.

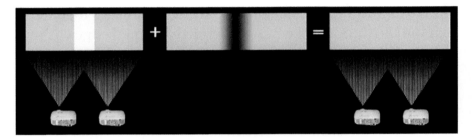

FIGURE 11.4
Applying blend zone.

Source: Roger Sodre

As illustrated above in Figure 11.4, the edge of each projected image is faded out so that the blend zone becomes equally as bright as the rest of the image. Again, there are a number of ways to do this. In many large venue projectors, there will be blending software built in. Many of them have built-in test patterns, which can be used to align the projectors to a known number of pixels, then setting that same number in the blending software. When doing this, the designer should communicate with the projectionist so that the proper blend zone is created.

The designer may also choose to create a blend using the media server. This is often the preferred method of the media server programmer. When they use their software, they are able to finish digitally aligning the grid as well as create the blend that exactly matches the content. As part of the initial planning process, the designer will need to know how the blend is going to be created and the capabilities of all of the equipment. While almost all blending software will have the ability to adjust the outer edges for an extra wide image, not all of them can blend for a taller image.

There is also the added challenge if the surface is not flat. Creating the blend zones for the mapped surface can be relatively straightforward as long as the blend still falls on a flat surface. Curved surfaces add only slightly more challenge, as the focal plane is not even. However, a domed surface can add quite a bit of challenge, as each piece of the image is divided like pie pieces.

One final note about blended images is that the projectors need to be closely matched. In an ideal world, the projectors will all be fairly new, of the same model, and with lamps of the same age. In the real world we get to choose the same model and that is about it. If working with your own gear, then you will be able to choose the projectors which are most closely matched and may even swap lamps to have them be similarly aged. No matter what, you will need to color match the projectors, as the audience will be more likely to see differences between them. Again, professional projectors are made for this purpose and often have the color matching built in and able to be fine-tuned. Consumer models will have some color temperature adjustment, which might get you close enough. It is recommended that if you are doing a large blend, do not rely on your eyes entirely, as they can become fatigued and be less reliable towards the end of the line. Similar to using light meters, and sometimes even in combination with them, the projectionist can use a device which will read specific color values of the primaries, which can be used to set specific values which are not up to interpretation.

As the majority of the images we produce will be bright and colorful, this is as far as the discussion needs to go for the majority of blended images. But, if we refer back to Figure 11.3, we see that, in the blend zone, the black levels are also increased. This will mostly be unnoticed by even trained projectionists while most content is being displayed. However, if the content has large areas of black, such as the alignment grid, then that grey area will be noticed. There is no way to bring those levels down, so instead we must bring the rest of the black levels up. Obviously, this reduces the overall contrast of the projection. However, if the black is going to be seen, then the designer will need to make the decision as to where the trade-off will be.

MOVING FIXTURES

Though it is not often used in theatrical settings, sometimes video content is projected through the use of moving fixtures. These will sometimes fall under the realm of the lighting designer and be referred to as digital lighting. There are a number of moving head fixtures that contain a projector instead of a traditional light source, with a mechanical means of changing the light coming out from it. Many of those same units will have a media player built into the base, which contains the content to be used. This can range from digital gobos to textural looping video to standard video clips. They are controlled by the lighting console.

In addition, some lighting manufacturers have created moving yoke systems, where a standard projector can be attached to it to perform a similar function. These projectors will benefit from a programmable lens system so that as the projector changes its position it can retain focus and may need to zoom.

Projectors manufactured for the rental/staging market will often accept DMX as part of their control functions.

Some projectors can be positioned in virtually any axis as required by the moving yoke, but some projectors may be too large or unable to be moved while operating. For those projectors, orbital head mirrors are sometimes sold as an attachment. Just as with orbital head moving lights, these are less popular for digital lighting. They have the advantage of being able to be used with a wider variety of projectors, so long as they can be attached. Also, the entire projector does not need to be visible, potentially allowing for use in more intimate spaces.

3D PROJECTION

There has been a repeating trend by filmmakers from the 1950s to the present to amplify viewer pleasure by attempting to make their movies more lifelike. One popular method, especially in modern cinema, is to have it appear three-dimensional. There have been a number of methods used to create this effect. They are generally split into two categories—active and passive. Both require eyewear. Engineers are still working on glasses-free applications, but as they are not currently viable, there is no need to discuss those theories.

Passive Optics

Various methods of passive optics have been the most often used method because of their availability for large-scale distribution. In the first few decades, the primary method of doing this was by using color filters—primarily red and blue. As this method can cause eye fatigue, the 3D effect is minimized. Also, this limits the projected image to monochrome. If this were to be used in a modern market, it would be for nostalgic purposes.

In modern cinema, adoption of polarized lenses has been successful enough to keep 3D alive for a number of years. For this application, two separate images are played on the screen simultaneously, with an image polarized 90 degrees opposite for the content intended to be seen from the left eye to the right eye. The glasses then are also 90 degrees out of polarity from one another, allowing each eye to only see its intended portion of the image.

This can be accomplished with standard projectors. To do so requires aligning the projectors in a stacked image configuration and fitting the appropriate polarizing filters in front of the lenses. Many large venue projectors are also 3D capable. When they are, as is the case in cinema applications, it is possible to use a single projector. These projectors do not require the external polarizing filter, as that is taken care of within the optics. They will generally use a higher frame rate, switching to essentially a normal frame rate as it alternates between showing the frame for the left eye and then the right eye.

The downside of using polarized filters for 3D viewing is that the brightness of the image is greatly diminished. In order to compensate, the content often is required to lose a lot of color range in order to keep it bright enough to register details. In addition, the viewing angle is reduced, which is less of a problem for cinema than it is for live theater.

As theater owners are looking for better solutions, projector manufacturers are happy to look for solutions. Enter the laser projector. While the laser phosphor projector may be able to be used for 2D content, it really takes the RGB, sometimes called three primary (3P), laser projectors to replace the Xenon projectors for polarized content. As the laser systems have a wider color gamut, they seem to offer better performance for keeping the image bright enough using the polarized system. However, manufacturers are also offering 6P laser projectors. There are two sets of primary colors used to create the full spectrum of visible light, far exceeding cinema standards for Xenon projectors. The glasses worn by the audience then filter one set of primaries or the other (kind of like the old red and blue), but these tend to not cause eye fatigue since they are full color range. This system offers the brightest passive 3D viewing experience with the best color performance. How much use it will get for the live entertainment market is yet to be seen. The cost may keep it in the cinema or theme parks for many years to come.

Active Shutters

While the eyewear for passive 3D systems are relatively inexpensive and can be somewhat expendable, the alternative is likely pricing itself out of existence. Active shutter glasses are mechanically driven to block vision from one eye to the other in series. This is timed to the playback of the content, which allows frames to be seen by the intended eye. As 3D TVs hit the mass market, this system was preferred by some owners, as they felt that the passive system was of poorer quality (brightness and color). However, the expense of purchasing additional eyewear and maintaining the system made it less desirable. Overall, in recent years at the Consumer Electronics Show, there have been fewer attempts at keeping the 3D market alive for home entertainment. In all honesty, this technology will likely not be the best decision by the media designer should there be a desire for 3D to be implemented in a production.

INTERACTIVE PROJECTION

While 3D may be the big selling point at the movies, having the set become alive with interactive projection is much more desired in live entertainment. With digital content, we have the flexibility of random access to information (as opposed to the linear nature of analog content) and have the flexibility of creating or compositing content in a live environment. This is finally allowing designers the ability to create the hybrid environment of the virtual and real that storytellers have desired for generations.

There is a difference between good choreography and actual interactive content. One requires a lot of rehearsal and relatively simple setup while the other allows freedom of movement but can be complicated when mounting the production. In any number of reality talent shows and live performances, there is inevitably an individual or group who has good enough timing to look as if the performer and projection are organically combined. As seen in Figure 11.5, in *The Beatles LOVE*, the dancers time their movements to arrive in specified areas to coincide with the change of the video content. This type of performance works best with music tracks so that the performers are better able to time their movements.

FIGURE 11.5
Dancers hitting their marks choreographed with content—The Beatles *LOVE*.

Source: Matt Beard

To be truly interactive is going to take more work on the designer's part. For effective application of interaction, the performer and image need to most often be in close proximity. If the performer is too far away from the image, there is a visible disconnect for the audience, which may forego the suspension of disbelief. This presents the challenge of how to keep the performer properly lit by the lighting designer while not having the image deteriorate from ambient light. The designer and director will need to determine if the projected image is acceptable on the performer or not. In addition, there needs to be a determination on how the rest of the choreography will take place, or what is acceptable to move away from the image. Finally, the designer needs to determine how to control the content.

Image Tracking

The primary intent of interactive projection is to have the content be able to respond to real life movement. For this to happen, the computer which controls interactive content needs to know where the object is which provides the interaction, as well as a way to identify that object. As seen in specials on computer generated images (CGI) for many Hollywood blockbuster movie, the performers will sometimes wear specialized suits covered in any number of markers, even on their faces. These markers are tracked by cameras, allowing software to use these real movements in a framework for creating something that lives in the virtual world. This can be utilized for live entertainment as well. After all, puppets have been used to entertain for centuries; we now have the ability to make virtual puppets through the same type of technology as used in Hollywood.

However, we have other needs of object tracking, including for props, which we want to have visible to the audience and not have the markers be visible. Some systems will use invisible infrared light to illuminate the markers in order to track them in front of the audience. These markers do not need to be very large, but need to be uncovered so that cameras around the performance space can see the reflection of the marker. The lighting of the overall performance may need to be dimmer so that the camera will see the reflectivity of the marker and not have errors caused by non-markers creating similar reflections. There are a few manufacturers that specialize in creating tracking systems which will work with the designer's choice of content, but these may be relegated to their media server.

Blob Detection

Not every production will have the means for image tracking systems, which can be costly. A simpler means of following an object which can be used for interactive video is blob detection. For our purposes, a blob is an amorphous object determined by a difference in an image captured by a camera. Often, the blob is the difference in luminance values as viewed by the camera. This requires a greater control of light and placement of the cameras in the performance space than with the optical markers. Floors that are too reflective, such as dance floors, may cause errant blob detection. If possible, narrowing the frequency of light to be detected will add accuracy.

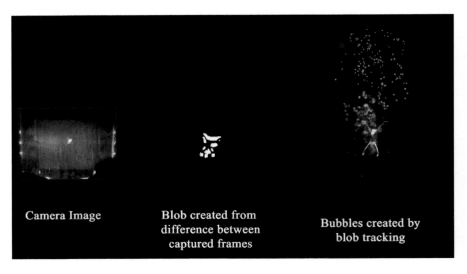

FIGURE 11.6
An effect created by blob detection.

Not every media server will have the ability to utilize this type of input. Those that do can use a number of means to obtain the blob. The computer will require a video capture card (internal or external devices are available) to bring in the live streaming of the video camera. It will need to convert the data coming in to a single type of data, generally a monochrome image to identify luminance variation. The designer will determine if an effect is created by movement, by a set luminance value, or possibly a combination of both. To track movement, the program must look at a difference between the frames.

Sensors

Precise control over the light is not always possible or practical. The designer can instead utilize a variety of sensors to detect the presence of a performer in order to create an interactive experience. There are a variety of mechanical and electrical means that can be used to identify and give data. Some of these devices will only provide a trigger, while others can give continuous feedback, allowing for variance in the effect created.

Sensors which provide momentary triggers will include motion detectors used in security lights or which open the doors at a local store. Unlike the motion tracking and blob detection previously mentioned, this does not provide continuous feedback. It will only be triggered based on set intervals within a defined field of view. This, along with switches such as pressure plates, is a common device used in fun houses and other interactive experiences for the audience. However, this does not preclude them for use in a performance setting.

Other sensors can provide constant, variable data, which is used differently by an interactive design. Instead of providing a momentary trigger, inductive sensors can identify varying amounts of pressure. This can potentially provide an intensity difference in an effect created, such as the difference in displacement a bowling ball or a child will have on a trampoline. Conversely, the same type of intensity difference can be created through a capacitance sensor. This is the type of sensor used in the screens of smart phones. As some may have found in colder climates, wearing gloves can cause unexpected results, no matter how hard the screen is pressed. This is because a capacitive sensor is relying on the interaction of an electrical field. Like the lights which appear to have Tesla coils inside them, where touching the outer glass will draw the electricity to someone's finger, the capacitive field will react similarly. The greater the amount of contact with an appropriate conductive object (the non-insulated human), the greater the interruption in the field. This can also provide varying amounts of data to be used by the designer. The benefit of capacitance over inductance is that it is possible to get an effect without actually touching the sensor, as smart phone users have inadvertently discovered when an app is triggered before they touch the screen.

Encoders

As introduced in Chapter 8, encoders are often employed by automation in order to receive data on the amount of travel and speed of set pieces. Often, the media designer does not need to employ additional encoders, but instead can network with the automation department to receive the positional data in order to track that set piece. While the automation department will be receiving absolute values in a linear position of the set, the media designer will need to interpret this data in three-dimensional space when using projection—less so if using an emissive display. The two effects often used in combination with the automated set are to either maintain the media with the surface or to give the illusion that the surface is a window, showing that which is hidden or giving the idea that the set is actually larger, but that the audience is only perceiving a part of the total world.

Particle Generation and Cellular Automatons

An interactive part of the design can trigger a pre-rendered clip by a momentary cue, change an element within the image, or may create a wholly new image. When a pre-rendered effect is triggered, this is essentially giving the power of the GO button to the performer. On the other hand, it is possible to have the performer trigger an effect which will be different every time it is engaged. There are a number of graphic tools that can be utilized.

A particle generator is a system that uses graphic particles (3D models, sprites, or other graphic objects) and creates "chaotic" phenomena. In a NLE, these are often employed to create smoke, fire, water, dust, or other amorphous objects which can enhance a rendered clip. For a live performance, this may be able to replace a physical effect which may not be able to be controlled properly or can be expensive. They can also provide a whimsical effect, as seen in Figure 11.7, where a clone of the observed target was transformed into a snow person. For this particular effect, the longer the target stayed still, the greater the accumulation of particles and the generation of larger particles. As the target would move, the particles would fall off.

257

Another tool is known as cellular automatons. These are discrete graphical units which interact with other cells within a given proximity. The particle generation system creates individual, predefined graphic units which operate among a set of rules, and they do not react with one another. The cellular automatons also follow a finite set of rules, but those rules include others within their "neighborhood". So these particles are able to create much more defined images which may appear more realistic. These can be arranged in density fields which can give more natural volume to the object. Game developers will use this technique to create more natural environments, and it is possible for the live entertainment designer to do the same.

FIGURE 11.7
Particle generation.

While particle generation has been implemented in a number of media server programs, the use of cellular automatons will require some true programming.

HOLOGRAPHY

Spectral illusions have been the desire of live entertainment for hundreds of years, from the early use of magic lanterns. Recently, they have been used to bring back celebrities from the grave (not literally) as well as create magical effects in theme parks. While these are not truly holograms, they are still ghostly images that resemble the effect. While live performance has not yet achieved the iconic effect simulated in the first *Star Wars* movie, researchers are getting closer. Until then, there are a few methods that the media designer can employ.

Pepper's Ghost

While the effect bears his name, John Henry Pepper was not the inventor of Pepper's Ghost. Instead, a man named Henry Dirks created the Dirksian Phantasmagoria in the middle of the nineteenth century. He brought a model of it to Pepper, who made some intuitive changes and was ultimately given lasting credit for the effect. Though this process has been known and used since then, from carnivals to Teleprompters, it came roaring back when it was used with video projection at the Coachella Music Festival.

To accomplish this effect, we are using both the reflective and transparent properties of a material (glass, for example). In a sense, this works similarly to the theatrical scrim, where we are controlling the light for what the audience will be able to see. We often see this at night when we have a brightly lit room and attempt to look outside, seeing our reflection in the glass, but beyond the glass, see only certain well-lit objects under the streetlight.

Traditionally, this effect is not created with video, but the more spectacular effects which are often shared on the internet most certainly are, and have many similarities. For a performance such as Coachella, the audience needed to be set back from the stage. This is where the magic happens. Projectors are aimed at a surface flat on the ground, unseen by the audience. The light which reflects off that surface is again reflected by an angled piece of transparent film (similar to Mylar without the reflective coating), which creates the secondary reflection that the audience sees. Just like what is required for you to see your reflection at night, the area behind the image needs to be relatively dark. The subject that will be interacting with the ghost will be off to the side. The media designer will have to work closely with the lighting designer for this to work. Most front light will be completely eliminated, as it would reflect off of the film, ruining the effect. The performers behind the film will be required to be mostly sidelit.

Light Field Display

Light travels in rays and in all directions. We use light often in a finite way. When we capture an image with a camera, we are restricted by a depth of field which the camera can have in focus. The future may hold some unexpected results. New light field cameras are able to get beyond some of these limitations. This allows for the unyielded capture of content, which allows for the adjustment of aperture, change of focal points, and so much more, when using the content. This means that the content is almost a virtual hologram. The designer will have the ability to manipulate living images.

Atmospheric Projection

Using the optical properties of Mie scattering, media designers will often use atmospheric effects to produce an image for the audience. At some attractions centered around man-made lakes, fine mist water fountains are used as rear projection surfaces. This often requires a fairly bright projector for the effect to be seen. Also, the water does not provide a particularly even surface, which can work in favor of the designer in some instances. As this will not be practical at many venues, let us look at what might be used.

It is possible to still use water even in a theatrical venue. There are manufacturers of ultrafine mist systems which can be placed over an area and keep the area under it relatively dry. The mist does require controlled airflow, as it can be easily dissipated. Even with a high degree of control, the mist only provides a relatively even surface for a few feet below the mechanism. The benefit is that this allows performers to walk through the projected image. It works best as a rear projected image and does require planning as to the placement of the projector.

Though the image will be displayed on the mist, much of the light goes directly through it, creating the ultimate hot spot. This means that the projector needs to be off axis, often above or below where it will be seen. However, the rest of the light will end up somewhere and you will have a perfect image that needs to be hidden.

Besides water mist, there are methods of directing theatrical smoke into a projection surface. Again, this will require a great deal of control over the air movement in the space and there will be a great amount of light wasted, which needs to be dealt with. The benefit of the fog systems is that they can be positioned in more orientations than just above. As they can direct the fog up, to the side, or down, there are more options for including them in set pieces.

LARGE-SCALE IMAGING

Going beyond the theater, many projection designs have been taken to famous buildings, from castles to the Sydney Opera House. These are scaled-up versions of projection mapping, which we previously discussed. The bigger challenge is that the designer will be working with materials of varying reflectance and colors. The thing that gives the designer the most freedom is that there is not the disconnect of scale, while in a traditional performance environment there is the possibility that the projection will be too great, ultimately upstaging the performers. With large-scale imaging, the video is the performance.

AUGMENTED REALITY

Projection mapping, in its own right, is spatial augmented reality. This is the process of taking an everyday object and altering reality through the use of video. However, augmented reality also takes on a virtual world when we use a camera and view the real world which is augmented with virtual elements on a screen. The consumer market was introduced to this with

Google Glass, where information could be provided to the user over special glasses. The concept started to gain some popularity with handheld games which provided markers in order to place virtual creatures on real objects. But, when the Pokémon Go app came out for smartphones, the general public started seeing where this might add some entertainment value.

For live performance, we may find that audiences will be more willing to try out viewing devices in order to enhance their experience. With the prevalence of smartphones and tablets being brought with the audience members, the media designer may look to encourage their use during a production. This will in all likelihood add one more member to the media team: the app programmer.

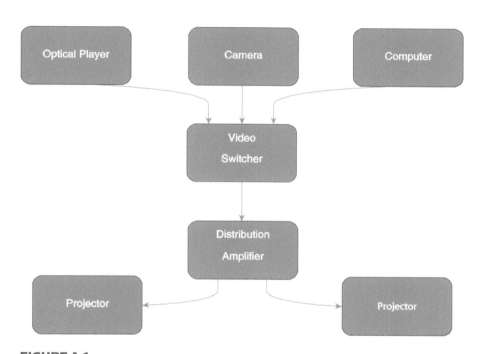

FIGURE A.1

Broadcast style design with multiple inputs, utilizing a switcher to go between inputs.

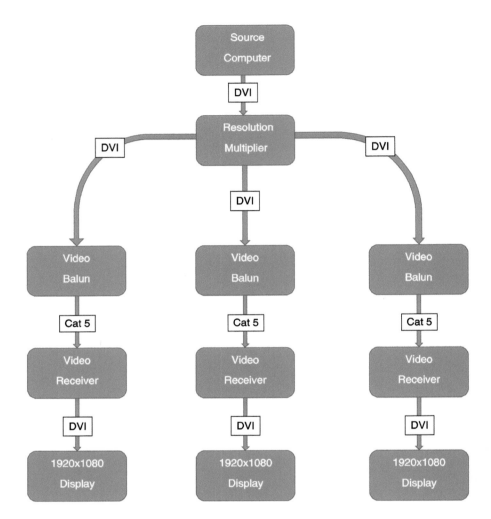

FIGURE A.2

A single source is able to drive multiple displays. Each display receives the same resolution. This example can drive three separate images. Replace the multiplier with a distribution amplifier, and the only difference is that all three displays would receive the exact same image.

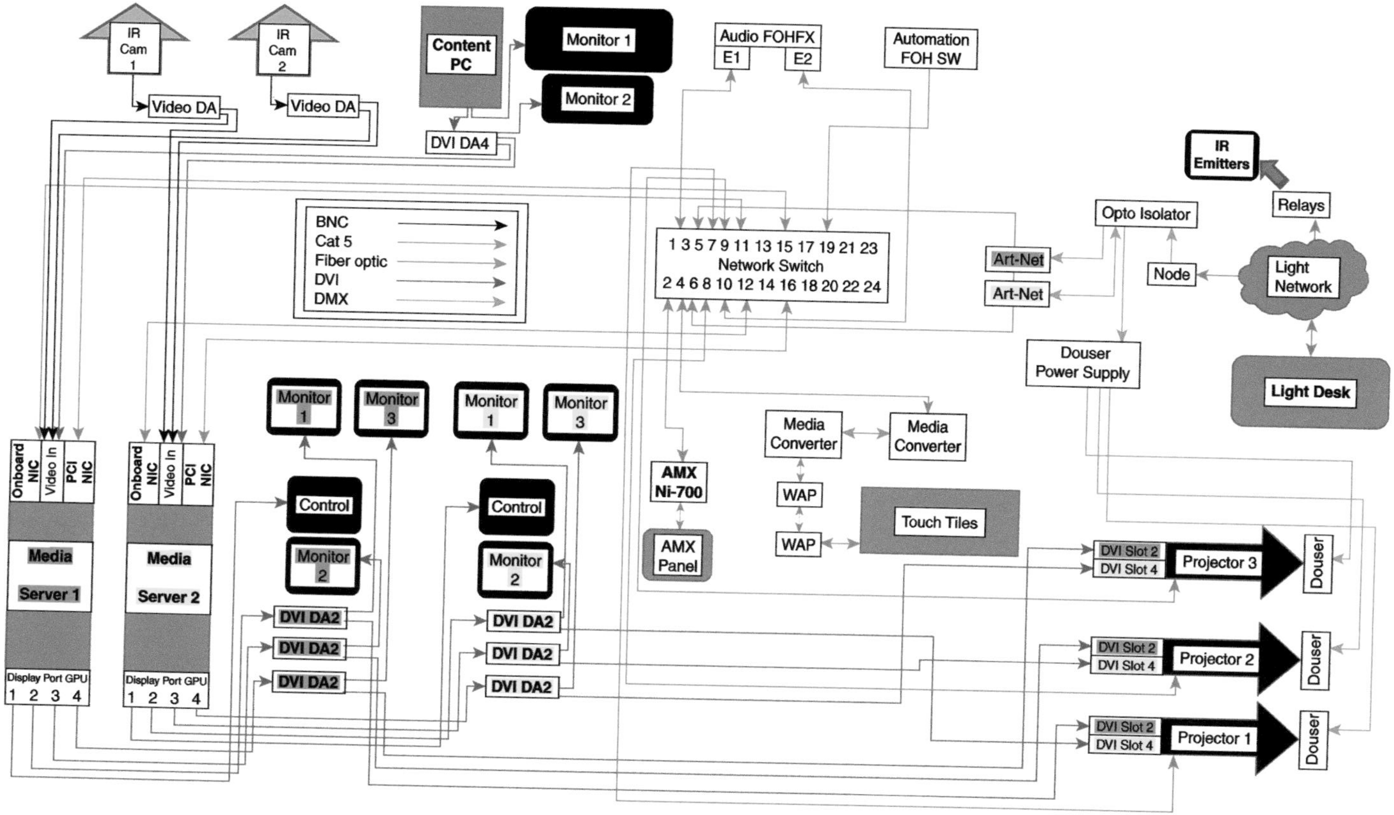

FIGURE A.3

A line drawing from a completed interactive design showing elements of source, distribution, network, control, and display. This system was designed with redundancy.

265

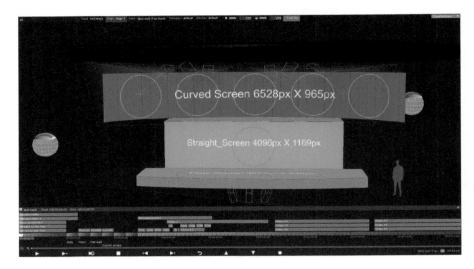

FIGURE A.4
Pre-visualization using D3.

Source: Shannon Harvey, Backstage Academy

Appendix B: Formulas

Screen Luminance (gain)
Output (lumens) – light loss (%) / screen area (ft^2) * gain = luminance (foot-lamberts)

Image Illuminance
Foot-lamberts = (lumens / screen area) * screen gain

Desired Contrast Ratio
Light output (lumens) = [(ambient light * desired contrast) * surface area] / 0.75 for derating

Measured Contrast Ratio
[La + (p * Lamb)] / [Lb + (p * Lamb)]

> La = *lumen output of projector divided by the surface area of the screen multiplied by the gain*

> Lb = *display black level*

> Lamb = *ambient light on surface, measured in foot-candles*

> p = 1.0 (*for front projection*) or 0.2 (*for rear projection*)

Minimum Light Output
Lumens = (9 * image area * p * Lamb) / (screen gain – 0.2)

Glossary

Additive Color Mixing: The process of using primary colors layered on top of one another in order to reach white. It is the process by which video projectors mix light.

Alpha Channel: A transparent portion of an image file; used when layering images in a projection.

Ambient Light: Unwanted light from sources other than the projector that radiate onto the projection surface. It negatively affects the contrast ratio of the projection.

Analog: The representation of an image through physical mechanisms such as a film projector.

Analog Signal: The transmission of data through physical quantities such as variations in voltage or magnetic polarization.

Analog Video: The process which uses a time-varying voltage that at any given moment is proportional to the chrominance and luminance of the corresponding pixel in the image.

ANSI Lumens: The standardized method of measuring luminous flux of a projected image as prescribed by the American National Standards Institute. This measures the averaged output of nine points on the projected image as opposed to the brighter center of the image.

Artifact: An unwanted element in a digital image that was not present at the time the content was recorded or rendered.

Art-Net: A method of communication developed by Artistic License for sending DMX data over an Ethernet network.

Aspect Ratio: The ratio of the width to the height of a raster. This is usually represented in ratio format, but it can also be represented as a decimal.

Auto Adjust: The process by which a display matches the signal being input. If the reference image is of poor quality, this may result in the adjustment not being set optimally.

Balun: An electronic device which converts a signal between balanced and unbalanced. As part of a video system, it is used to extend signals over a greater distance on a category cable than is possible with a standard cable.

Bandwidth: The frequency range of a transmission, as expressed in megahertz (MHz).

Bayonet Neill-Concelman (BNC): A terminal connection for co-axial cables which features a twisting lock outer ring. It is used on both analog and digital signals on professional grade equipment.

Bit: A zero or a one used in computers. This is the basic unit of digital data.

Bit Rate: The frequency at which bits are transmitted; referenced as bits per second.

Black Burst: A composite signal which carries only a black image, along with the horizontal and vertical sync, to be used as a reference signal.

Black Level: A measurement of the black portion of a video signal which represents zero units of color. For a measured analog signal, this should not go below 7.5 IRE (Institute of Radio Engineers) units.

Blanking: The process of replacing the chrominance and luminance values of a portion of a video signal with null values. This gives a black value for areas where the video signal is not desired.

Brightness: The subjective and non-scientific human perception of light used to arbitrarily describe the projected or emitted video image attributes. Factors that can contribute are the total number of lumens reflected to the viewer and the contrast ratio of the total projected image.

Broadcast: The group communication where data is sent to all destinations simultaneously.

Camera: A device for capturing still or sequential images. Digital cameras can communicate images in real time to other portions of a video system. A virtual camera is used in modeling programs to establish a viewpoint of a 3D model.

Category Cable: A cable bundle of four twisted pair wires used in computer networks; generally terminated with an RJ-45 (Registered Jack 45, un-keyed 8 position 8 contact) connector.

Chroma Key: A video process which removes a particular hue (chroma value) in order to layer video. The process is commonly known as "blue screen" or "green screen" and is used in cinema production and weather forecasts on television.

Chrominance: The color component of a video signal. Can be referred to as chroma.

Codec: A software component by which a video signal is compressed for storage and transport and decompressed for display.

Color Bars: A video test signal which provides the elements necessary for the visual setup of a display. The test pattern should include a white and black reference. as well as a hue reference to primary and secondary colors.

Color Depth: The number of bits of information used for the color information of a single pixel.

Color Gamut: The range of colors that can be produced by a display. It is referenced by the international standards body on illumination, Commission International de l'Eclairage (CIE). CIE 1931 is the most common reference to typical human eye response to color.

Color Temperature: A reference to the variance in white that is created by a light source; measured in Kelvin. Colors in the spectrum can be subjectively described as warm (reds and yellows) or cool (blues).

Component Video: An analog baseband signal which carries luminance and sync on a single co-axial cable, with the variances in red and blue carried on separate co-axial cables.

271

Composite Video Baseband Signal (CVBS): An analog, unmodulated video signal where all data is carried on a single co-axial video cable. It is often referred to as just "composite".

Compositing: The process by which multiple layers of video information are combined into a single video signal. This process is most often completed in a non-linear video editing program, but may also be completed live with the use of a media server.

Compression: Various means of reducing the size of a video file through the elimination of redundant data; used for storage and transport.

Container File: A media file containing compressed audio and video data. It may support multiple file formats and may or may not contain the same file extension as the file within.

Contrast Ratio: The mathematical ratio between the white and black portions of an image. It can be measured between full white to full black images (useful in determining the brightness of video black) or as the average between 16 alternating black and white rectangles (ANSI method).

Controller Interface Transport Protocol (CITP): A protocol which links lighting controllers with media systems.

Convergence: Alignment of the red, green, and blue components of a display system so that the colors can be blended for human vision.

Corner Pin: An advanced method of keystone correction by which the user is able to adjust the video image by digitally correcting where the four outer corners of the image are projected in relation to the surface intended.

Central Processing Unit (CPU): The circuitry in a computer that carries out the instructions of a program. The speed and power needed depends on how much computational power is required by the user for the number and complexities of programs being processed at any given time.

Decibel: A logarithmic comparison between two power measurements; used in determining the strength of a signal.

Decompression: The restructuring of a compressed video signal back to its original state in order to be used in a display. Redundant information which was originally discarded in the compression process is unrecoverable and is instead re-created by the rules established in the codec.

Digital Light Processing (DLP): A process developed by Texas Instruments which utilizes millions of tiny mirrors which oscillate back and forth in order to create digital images.

Digital Micromirror Device (DMD): A micro electro-mechanical series of mirrors which is the core component of a DLP system.

Digital Multiplexing: A protocol for lighting systems by which a lighting controller is able to exchange information to dimmers and other stage lighting equipment. Some video equipment is established to respond to this protocol as well.

Digital Signal: The transmission of a video signal through a series of binary bits, in the way computers transmit information.

Digital Video Disk (DVD): An optical disk storage system that was developed to contain 135 minutes of MPEG-2 standard definition compressed video at a resolution of up to 720x480.

Digital Video Interface (DVI): A serial protocol for delivering high definition uncompressed video using Transition Minimized Differential Signaling (TMDS); developed by the Digital Display Working Group (DDWG).

DisplayPort: A digital display interface developed by the Video Electronics Standards Association (VESA) which can connect a source with one or more digital displays. It is compatible with DVI and HDMI through the use of active and passive adapters.

Douser: A mechanical device which places a physical barrier between the light source and the display surface. This device is commonly an external accessory to a projector but may also be internal (referred to as a shutter). It is used to control video black output.

273

Edge Blending: A process by which multiple projected images are overlapped near the edges of each display to form a single, seamless image. The edges have repeated pixels and the overlapped area has a layer added to reduce the brighter areas where the blend occurs.

Ethernet: Computer networking technology used in Local Area Networks (LAN) and Wide Area Networks (WAN).

Extended Display Identification Data (EDID): A data structure developed by the Video Electronics Standards Association (VESA) which allows the display and source to share information regarding the capabilities of resolution and refresh rate of the display.

Extender: A device used to increase the range of distribution of a video signal beyond what is possible by standard means.

Field: In an interlaced video system, this represents one half of a scanned video image—either the odd or the even lines.

Fixed Lens: A lens which has a fixed focal length. When in a video projector, it requires repositioning of the equipment to change the size of a projected image.

Flash Memory: Digital data storage requiring no moving parts.

Focal Length: The distance from the lens of a projector to where the collimated beam of light is brought to a focal point.

Foot-Candle: The primary unit of illumination measurement representing the intensity of a square foot surface as lit by a standard candle one foot away.

Foot-Lambert: The unit of measuring luminance as lumens per square foot (when the light is Lambertian).

Frame: One complete still video image. It can consist of two fields.

Frame Rate: The frequency with which individual image frames are displayed. It is listed as frames per second.

Front Projection: The process by which the projector is on the same side of the screen surface as the audience. The projected image is reflected on the screen to be viewed.

Gain: In terms of a front projection screen, this is a measurement made perpendicular from the center of the surface of the luminance reflected by the screen, divided by the luminance radiating from the projector.

Gamma Correction: An adjustment parameter for the luminance of a video signal. In a non-Cathode Ray Tube (CRT) display, it will accommodate for gamma encoded in the signal intended for the CRT display.

Generator Locking (Genlock): Frame synchronization using a specific video reference signal from a signal generator, such as black burst.

Graphics Processing Unit (GPU): An electronic circuit designed to accelerate the creation of images in a frame buffer to be output to a display.

Hard Disk Drive (HDD): A data storage device for computers which stores the data on magnetic spinning disk. Data read and write speeds are determined by the speed at which it spins.

High Definition: Video signals which exceed standard definition as defined by television standards; generally displayed in 16:9 aspect ratio.

High Definition Multimedia Interface (HDMI): A digital multimedia interface which carries both audio and video information using Transition Minimized Differential Signaling (TMDS) and contains content protection.

IEEE 1394: An interface standard for rapid transit of audio and video information developed by the Institute of Electrical and Electronics Engineers (IEEE) working group. It is also known as FireWire (Apple), i.LINK (Sony), and Lynx (Texas Instruments).

Infrared: A portion of the electromagnetic spectrum which has longer wavelengths than is perceived by humans. Most thermal radiation (heat) comes from this portion of the spectrum. As it is not visible to humans, it can be used for invisible light wave communication as well as tracking motion with cameras.

Interlace Scanning: The process of reducing the amount of bandwidth in a video signal by using two fields of alternating lines of data to create a single frame of video.

Illuminance: The density of light on a surface. One lumen of light evenly distributed over one square meter will result in the luminance of one lux.

Joint Photographic Experts Group (JPEG): A defining body which developed a popular image compression scheme using the same acronym. The image compression divides still images into blocks to compress them with discrete cosine transformation. It is a lossy format with a higher compression ratio, which degrades the quality of the image.

Keystone: Optical distortion of a projected image when the projector and screen are not perpendicular to the center line.

Lamp: The optical unit consisting of a bulb and housing which provides illumination for a projector.

Layer: A video element used in editing and media servers to mix images.

Lens: The optical component used to focus a projected image; available in a variety of focal lengths as well as varifocal lengths.

Lens Shift: A feature which allows some projectors to move the lens in order to make an adjustment of the placement of the projected image.

Lenticular: A texture on a screen surface which affects the performance of reflected and transmitted light to alter viewing angle.

Letterbox: A blanking area on the top and bottom of an image used when the content is of a wider aspect than the display.

Light Emitting Diode (LED): A semiconductor which has the ability to create a narrow frequency of light. LEDs are relatively bright, use little power, and create low heat.

Liquid Crystal Display (LCD): A digital image creation device using liquid crystals to modulate light through polarized filters.

Liquid Crystal on Silicon (LCOS): Also known as D-ILA (JVC) and SXRD (Sony), this places an LCD panel over a reflective surface to create a digital image.

Long Throw Lens: A projector lens designed for long focal lengths.

Lossless Compression: The restored image is an exact duplicate of the original image without the loss of any data. This results in larger file sizes.

Lossy Compression: The restored image is an approximation of the original image, as some data is lost or discarded during the compression sequence.

Luma: The encoded luminance in a video signal. When combined with chroma, a complete color image is produced. Without chroma, this produces a black and white image.

Lumen: A unit of luminous flux of one candela; used to measure the total amount of visible light emitted.

Luminance: The measurement of lumens per unit in a projected area, expressed in foot-lamberts.

Mapping: A process of using software to alter a projected image to conform to a three-dimensional object.

Masking: A process of using software to blank out portions of a displayed image in undesired areas.

Media Server: A computer device or program designed for manipulating video and audio files in real time for live performance.

Metadata: Information that is added to a serial data stream which provides data about the image and audio files.

Mirroring: Sending the same video signal to remote displays as is displayed on the source computer.

Moiré: A type of digital artifact which causes angled or curved lines to appear. The difference in frequency depends on the individual patterns and harmonics.

Multiple Display Adapter: An intermediary device which allows the single output of a source computer to be expanded to multiple devices by creating a larger raster. Display devices should all match in native resolution, as the adapter essentially doubles or triples the width of the initial display, maintaining the same aspect ratio.

Multicasting: The group communication where data is sent to multiple destinations simultaneously.

Musical Instrument Digital Interface (MIDI): A communication protocol used between devices in order to control one another.

Native Resolution: The actual number of pixels that a display produces; based on the number of pixels on the image creating device.

Network: The use of Ethernet connected devices to easily exchange data.

Nit: A unit of luminous measurement equaling one candela per square meter. It is generally used for emissive sources, though it can be used in a projected display as well.

Opacity: A measure of transparency of an image within the digital realm. It is used when fading between images or combining elements. An alpha channel has areas with opacity of 100 and other areas with opacity of 0 (invisible areas).

Open Sound Control (OSC): A protocol for control communication between multimedia devices.

Overlay: The addition of computer generated graphics on top of a still or motion video.

Packets: Segments of a data stream in an internet protocol.

Persistence of Vision: A period of time for which the retina retains an image. This allows for sequential images to appear as moving images and allows the eye to see mixed colors from a video display.

Pillared: When an image has a narrower aspect ratio than the display, blanking occurs on the sides of the image.

Pixel: The acronym for picture element, which is the smallest element in a displayed image.

Pixel Density: The measurement of a number of pixels in a given area.

Pixel Pitch: The distance between pixels in an emissive display, measured from the center of each. Distance is measured in millimeters.

Pixelation: Distortion of an image which is improperly scaled, where the image loses clarity as data is repeated, looking like blocks.

Primary Color: A color which cannot be subdivided. In light, the three primaries are red, green, and blue.

Progressive Scan: The process by which a video image is recorded and displayed as full frames in sequence.

Projection Axis: The position of a projector to its display surface. Ideally, this will be a perpendicular relationship.

Pulldown: The process by which film at 24 fps is converted to video at 30 fps.

Random Access Memory (RAM): The working memory of a computer system; used for frequent storage for program instructions.

Raster: The display area of device. It was originally intended as the area for an individual device, but can also describe the area of all devices working together for a single display. It is measured in the pixels used to create the image.

RCA connector: A compression connector for a co-axial cable; developed by the Radio Corporation of America. It is most often used in consumer electronics.

Real Time: The transfer of data at a rate in which processing happens with little to no latency.

Rear Projection: The process by which the projector is on the opposite side of the surface than the audience. The image is transmitted through a translucent screen material.

Render: The process by which an editing program generates an image from a model or image file.

Resolution: The total number of pixels in a given area, as represented by rows and columns.

Router: A device for directing data. In a video system this allows for multiple inputs to be directed to a number of displays or a single input to multiple displays. In a computer network, this is a specialized switch which allows a bridge between networks.

Saturation: The amount of color data as a ratio of luma and chroma.

Scaling: Changing the resolution of a video file to fit the display.

Scan Converting: Converting the refresh rate and format of a video signal to match the display.

Screen: A specialized projection surface which has been created with researched materials in order to provide a predictable area for the optimum projected image.

Secondary Color: The three colors which are a direct combination of two primary colors and exactly the opposite of the third primary. The three colors are cyan, magenta, and yellow, and are often used in subtractive color mixing in light and printing.

Serial Advanced Technology Attachment (SATA): An interface used to connect components such as a hard drive to the motherboard of a computer.

Serial Digital Interface (SDI): First standardized by SMPTE (the Society of Motion Picture and Television Engineers), it is a video transmission protocol used to transmit uncompressed, unencrypted digital video over co-axial cable using a BNC connection. There are a number of standards depending on the level of data to be transmitted. Higher bandwidth versions allow for high definition serial data to be transmitted. This is not available in consumer equipment.

Solid State Drive (SSD): A data storage device that uses flash memory and thus has no moving parts like an HDD. It has a much faster read-write speed.

Subtractive Color Mixing: The process by which mixing secondary colors brings the end result towards black. This is used in electrowetting displays, printing, and theatrical moving lights.

Surface: A physical medium which will have projected light. In some playback software, this is the designation of where video will be directed when controlling multiple outputs.

S-Video: The separation of the chroma and luma in an analog video signal.

Switcher: In a video system, this allows for multiple inputs to be switched between for a single display. In a computer system, this is a device which allows communication of multiple connected devices within a LAN.

Test Pattern: An image with a specified pattern of colors, gridded lines, and other elements, used to optimize a display. When using multiple displays, it can be used for image blending, color matching, and brightness matching.

Thin-Film Transistor (TFT): A technology where each pixel has its own transistor switch in an Active Matrix LCD panel.

Throw Distance: The distance between the projector and surface required to make a specific size image.

Throw Ratio: The ratio of the distance between the projector and the surface width. This is used to determine the position of the projector and the lens required to make a specified image size.

Timecode: A coding system by which different pieces of equipment can work together through synchronized operations. There is a single generator that is transmitted to the connected devices.

Transcoding: The process by which one video format is converted to another as needed by the playback devices.

Transmittance: The rear projection luminance factor measuring the ability of the surface to pass projected light through the screen. Compare to gain for a front projection system.

Unicast: The group communication where data is sent to a single destination.

Universal Serial Bus (USB): The cables, connectors, and communications protocols used for bus communication between computers and electronic devices.

Unshielded Twisted Pair (UTP): An inexpensive cable, usually 22 or 24 American Wire Gauge, used in many Ethernet networks. It is often used with video baluns. UTP is allowed for cable construction up to category 6.

Vector Graphics: A computer graphics system which uses polygons to represent images based on vectors. Various fonts are the most common form of vector graphics.

Video Black: The value sent to a display with chroma and luma at zero. This is the amount of light which is still present in a display when those values are received.

Video Card: An accessory appliance in a computer system dedicated to production of video output. Processing and speed is greatly improved over an integrated video system.

Video Graphics Array (VGA): Specifically, this is the video signal with a resolution of 640x480. Commonly, this term is used to describe any analog signal which is transferred over a cable using a 15-pin connector (DE-15).

Video Random Access Memory: A component of a video card which acts as the framebuffer memory between the CPU and the GPU. Greater amounts will allow a computer to process a greater amount of video data without slowing down the system.

Viewing Angle: The angle from the center of the screen where the brightness is halved.

Visible Spectrum: A portion of the electromagnetic spectrum visible to the human eye. The typical person can see a range of about 390–700nm. Video displays attempt to reach this range, but cannot quite make it.

Zoom Lens: Also known as a varifocal lens, this is a projection lens which offers a greater range of the size of a projected image while placed in a single place. There will be some extra loss of light as compared to a fixed focus lens.

Index